Business Success With Ease

Top experts share strategies for accelerated growth

THRIVE Publishing
A Division of PowerDynamics Publishing, Inc.
San Francisco, California
www.thrivebooks.com

ISBN: 978-0-9897129-0-3

Library of Congress Control Number: 2013952822

Printed in the United States of America on acid-free paper.

URL Disclaimer: All Internet addresses provided in this book were valid at press time.
However, due to the dynamic nature of the Internet, some addresses may have changed
or sites may have changed or ceased to exist since publication.

We Dedicate This Book to You...

the intrepid business owner, sales professional or consultant, whether you are experienced or are just starting out on your path to entrepreneurship. You recognize the power of knowing what to do and when to do it—you are ready to grow your business with ease. We salute you for taking action and we celebrate your commitment to becoming the best you can be.

The Co-Authors of *Business Success with Ease*

Table of Contents

Acknowledgements

Gratitude is an important part of business success. Before we share our wisdom and experience with you, we have a few people to thank for turning our vision for this book into a reality.

This book is the brilliant concept of Caterina Rando, the founder of Thrive Publishing™ and a respected business speaker and strategist. Over the years Caterina has shown us all how much value we have to share. She has motivated us in our own businesses; she has helped us grow with ease. Caterina also inspired us to share our knowledge and experience so you, our reader, can also learn and thrive. Without her "take action" spirit, positive attitude and commitment to excellence, you would not be reading this book of which we are all so proud.

Diligence is also an important part of business success. We would also like to thank our dedicated team for their tireless efforts in making *Business Success with Ease* the best book it could be. We are grateful for everyone's stellar contribution.

To Susan Rich who served as project manager and lead editor for this book, we appreciate her patient guidance, thoughtful advice and genuine enthusiasm for our work, and we are truly grateful.

To Tammy Tribble and Noël Voskuil, our designers extraordinaire, who brought their creative talents to the cover and book layout, thank you both for your enthusiasm, problem solving and attention to detail throughout this project.

To Karen Gargiulo and Rua Necaise who provided us with keen proofreading eyes, thank you for your support and contribution and for making us read so perfectly on paper.

The Co-Authors of *Business Success With Ease*

Introduction

Congratulations! You are about to immerse yourself in an incredible resource; you are about to discover how to grow your business with ease. We joined together to write this book because we once stood where you are today—entrepreneurs with an amazing idea, seeking expert advice to carry us forward. Now we are ready to share with you how we—successful entrepreneurs—use innovative business strategies and today's online, high-tech world to achieve lasting business growth.

In the following pages, we will explain how to create a solid foundation for your business. Then we eliminate your phone call phobia so you can set—and achieve—stellar sales goals. We will reveal nine rules for excellent customer service and how live events connect you with more clients. Personal relationships are the hallmark of today's successful business owner. We will tell you how to use social media to your best advantage—like forging powerful connections on LinkedIn®, effective blogging strategies and using eBay® to position your service-based business.

There is a wealth of information here and we understand it can be overwhelming at first. We recommend you read the book once, cover to cover, then go back and follow the advice that applies to you and where you are today. Tomorrow, next week or next quarter, you will be ready for the next step, and all the ones after that, that build your business with ease.

Ideas in themselves are not transformative—they need to be paired with intention. Take the action. Take our advice. Ask us for help. We are confident that with our knowledge and your commitment, your business will thrive.

The Co-Authors of *Business Success With Ease*

Experts

Strategies

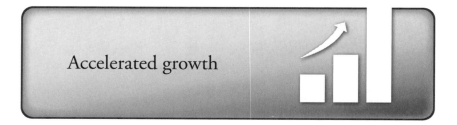

Accelerated growth

The Basic Steps that Help Grow Your Business with Ease

By Candy Messer

As an entrepreneur, you may have started a business for any number of reasons. Perhaps you were laid off and wanted to try owning your own business, maybe you had a hobby you turned into products or services you sell, or maybe you see it as freedom to be your own boss. No matter why you started your own company, you may be making some mistakes that stop you from growing with ease. Most of these errors can impact the financial success of your business. Here is what to look for and how to set your business up so it operates with ease.

> *"Regulations grow at the same rate as weeds."*
> **—Norman Ralph Augustine, American author**

Compliance Issues

As a business owner, there are many regulations you are required to follow. Numerous government agencies require registration and fees to operate legally. Research your city, state and federal guidelines to make sure you are following the rules. Here are some tips to help you stay in compliance.

• Get the proper licenses and/or permits.
Depending on your industry, there can be quite a few licenses or permits that are required. Make sure you are legally operating in your city by applying for a business license and paying the applicable fees. Licenses are renewed annually and the fees can be based on any number of different criteria. Some charge by the income level, some by the type of work, and some by the number of employees. If you are working from home, check to see if you need a special permit.

If you are selling tangible property, a seller's permit to collect and remit sales tax is required. This permit also allows you to purchase materials used in the final product without paying sales tax on the purchases. There are often additional permits required for certain industries such as those selling tobacco, alcohol, fuel, products that result in hazardous waste (including electronics) and others. And for those operating food establishments, the health department must inspect and issue a certificate before the business can open.

• Calculate sales tax—properly.
Most states have sales tax, and many have multiple levels as a result of voters approving increases for their cities and counties. If products are delivered directly to your customer, you apply the tax rate based on the location of your customer. Not charging the customer correctly for purchases means your business will be required to pay any uncollected sales tax. Contact your state sales tax agency to find out rates for cities where your products are sold. Properly calculate, collect and remit these taxes when due.

• File required paperwork—on time!

There are due dates for estimated tax payments, payroll and sales taxes, licenses and more. Educate yourself on deadlines that apply to your business to avoid late filing penalties and interest. Depending on the amounts due, deadlines may be monthly, quarterly or annually. I suggest writing these dates on your calendar with reminders so they are not easily missed. Late filing penalties are often 10 percent of the amount due plus interest—this can have a serious impact on the cash flow of your business.

• The 1099 is your friend, not foe.

As a business owner, you are mandated by the Internal Revenue Service (IRS) to file 1099 forms annually. Who gets a 1099? As a general rule, vendors you have paid who are not incorporated—with a few exceptions—more than $600 during the course of a year. Why is this important? Minus the 1099, the IRS might assume you, the solo business owner, have employees, not vendors. That means you will owe employee taxes, including social security. You might also get charged with other penalties. Protect yourself—get in the habit of filing 1099's for every person you do business with who qualifies to receive a form. One other exception to the rule: if you have paid your vendor by credit card, do not issue a 1099 as they will receive one from their credit card processor.

In order to properly file these forms, it is necessary to have the vendor's legal business name, address, and tax identification number. To get this information, a W9 form is first sent to the vendor to complete and return. I recommend that you not pay your vendor until this form has been returned to you.

This is a complicated topic, be sure to ask your bookkeeper for proper guidance and support.

Keeping Your Books with Ease

You have many things to consider when it comes to keeping your records and analyzing the data to improve your success. Newer business owners often make mistakes that complicate their book-keeping and create unnecessary challenges during tax season or if they need a bank loan. Avoiding—or fixing—these mistakes will greatly improve the prosperity of your company.

• **Do not mix business and personal funds.**
As an entrepreneur, you may feel using personal bank and credit card accounts for business transactions is easier—and possibly less expensive—than using business accounts. However, it is essential to have separate accounts for many reasons. When business trans-actions are paid with personal funds, the bookkeeping is more difficult. When business and personal transactions are combined, you are required to track which are true business expenses. Then you have to capture those properly for the tax return. Reconciling a combined statement can be much more time consuming than setting up a business and personal account.

More importantly, in case of an audit, it is likely that combined expenses will be disallowed. If it cannot be easily determined that these are a true business expense, the deduction will be deemed personal (this raises your overall tax burden). The IRS may also see your business as a hobby and deductions are not allowed for hobbies. If your business is an entity—that means you are an LLC, an S Corp or a C Corp, you do not want to pierce the corporate veil. As an entity, there is built-in protection from your personal assets in case of litigation. However, if funds have been mixed, the separation between business and personal is seen to not exist, and your personal assets may be used in the case of a judgment against you.

Another benefit of having a business account is that you will appear much more professional if paying with a business check or credit card than a personal account. Having checks written to a business name rather than your own gives more credibility as well.

• Avoid poor cash flow.

If you are just getting started, I encourage you to look at cash flow and your budget often. Cash flow is tricky—to profitably run your business, you need to know how much money you need to open the doors, then how long it will take to generate revenue. One common problem is over-estimating income and under-estimating expenses. This means you spend more money than you are making and it can lead to serious cash flow issues. The goal is to correctly estimate your profitability so you have enough capital available to run your business until you achieve positive cash flow. Sometimes this can take years; be sure you have access to cash or credit to tide you over.

> *"Small businesses have told us that having cash in their pocket*
> *is one of the primary things that they need."*
> **—Karen Mills, American public servant**

Do you know the easiest way to improve cash flow? Invoice consistently. If you plan to invoice when projects are complete, send the invoice as soon as the work is done. If your billing cycle is scheduled on a certain day of the month, make sure the invoices go out that day, every month. Arrange your schedule—or your bookkeeper's—to make this happen. Too many times I have seen business owners "too busy getting the work done" to send out their invoices. Your clients will not pay you if you do not invoice them. If you do not invoice timely, your clients are not going to think it is important to pay you on time. This can have a significant impact on your cash flow.

To improve cash flow, set up terms for customer invoices that will bring money into your business quickly. If you sell a product, this may not apply, as you are most likely paid when customers make a purchase. However, service-based businesses often bill after work has been completed. You can have payment due upon receipt of invoice, or a set number of days from the date of the invoice, like five, ten or fifteen. I do not recommend anything over thirty days. Keep in mind some customers will pay much later than your provisions, therefore an invoice with thirty-day terms may not be paid for forty-five days or more.

Manage your cash flow by requiring a deposit, with the balance due upon completion. Watch your cash flow carefully and make sure you plan for upcoming expenses so you have the money to pay them on time. Failure to watch your cash flow can mean your business fails due to lack of funds.

Budgeting is also critical. I encourage you to create a budget and stick to it as best as possible. Look at your income and your upcoming expenses. If you do not have enough sales, what expenses can be reduced? If you are just starting out, it may be difficult to come up with accurate figures for the income and expenses. I recommend you set up a budget, look at it frequently and adjust as necessary. Once you have finished your first year in business, use the prior year's figures, with any adjustments necessary, to come up with a budget for the upcoming year.

• **Price items correctly.**
When setting prices, consider all the costs incurred to develop and sell the product, including overhead such as rent, insurance and utilities. Whether it is a product or service, consider more than just the cost of materials and the mark-up you would like to earn.

Take the time to analyze your costs—avoid picking a number hoping it will be enough to bring about profitability. There are various pricing strategies out there—discount pricing means you charge less than your competitor. You will have to sell more volume to make up for the less expensive pricing. You can also position yourself as an industry leader, in which case you will charge more for your products and services. You will likely have fewer customers and will have to invest more in your marketing efforts. Outside of that, take into consideration the administrative time required to run the business that is not directly billable to your client. When setting prices, make sure you consider all expenditures and determine what margin is required to operate profitably.

I suggest finding a coach or mentor who is familiar with your industry and can give you tips on how to determine pricing, as well as other best practices for your industry. Learning what and what not to do early on will help you increase sales and reduce expenses.

- **Learn the basics of bookkeeping.**
As a newer business owner, you may be doing the bookkeeping yourself—that is fine, just make sure you are posting your transactions correctly. You may not have taken accounting courses and possibly do not understand the proper way to track income, expenses and other types of transactions. You may be so busy doing the work that you are unable to take the time to do your bookkeeping consistently. When tax time rolls around, you may quickly grab your paperwork and try to get the bookkeeping done well enough to give the information to the CPA. Perhaps you post all money in as income and all money out as expenses. This generally is not accurate, as deposits may include sales tax which is a liability, not income. Payments may be reducing liabilities (loans, taxes due). If you are doing your own bookkeeping, it is imperative to have a basic understanding of accounting principles

and how to apply them to your business. Learn the basics so you know the health of your business.

• Reconcile all accounts.
The balance sheet shows all assets, liabilities and equity of the business. One common mistake busy business owners make is only reconciling the main bank account. They do this because smaller accounts do not have as many transactions, and the thinking is, *I can remember that.* I challenge you to reconcile every bank, loan and credit card statement each month.

Improper posting of transactions will not be caught if statements are not reconciled on a monthly basis. It can also mean that you fail to capture all expenses. For instance, if you are not reconciling your credit card statement, some expenses may not be included such as purchases or finance charges not added to the credit card balance. Should your business need a loan, the balance sheet will be requested. A balance sheet with accounts that have not been reconciled could keep you from securing the loan or a line of credit.

Hire an Expert—Grow with Ease

You may have come to the realization that it is in your best interest to hire someone to help you with specific business tasks and that is great. My advice here is to hire experts. While you may be looking to spend the least amount of money to preserve cash flow, the cheapest choice often does not have the right experience or deliver the best outcome.

For example, if you need a bookkeeper, hiring someone who is not an expert can mean your books are done incorrectly and you will have to pay someone else to fix them—generally at a much higher rate. It is more cost effective to find someone who knows how to do the work from the start to make sure your information is accurate.

One of the advantages of hiring an expert is the valuable information he or she provides to you about your business. You will get reports that show your profitability—this helps you understand where changes need to be made to improve your business. An experienced bookkeeper is not one of those things you have to pay for, like business cards. This person is a member of your team who provides valuable information necessary for the success of your business.

Conclusion

There are a lot of steps that go toward building your business with ease. It is important that you comply with local, state and federal agencies and are keeping accurate records for tax purposes and business funding. You may feel overwhelmed, just keep in mind there are experts who can help you thrive in this endeavor.

Candy Messer

**Affordable Bookkeeping
and Payroll Services, Inc.**

Call us today, have peace of mind tonight!

310-534-5577
contact@abandp.com
www.abandp.com

Candy Messer is a bookkeeping and payroll expert who works with entrepreneurs in service-based industries such as fast food services, medical offices, landscaping and interior design. She energizes business owners by removing the burden of the bookkeeping and payroll processing. As a result of using her services, her clients have peace of mind and the freedom to do what they love. With more than 15 years of experience, Candy understands the stresses business owners face and offers customized services to meet their varying needs, including bookkeeping, payroll, Quickbooks™ consulting and bill pay services.

Candy speaks on topics such as what to know before hiring an employee, the benefits of outsourcing services, and how to become financially savvy. Candy was named Woman of the Year for 2009-2010 by the Peninsula Chapter of the American Business Women's Association. She was named the 2011 Entrepreneur Mom of the Year by *Today's Innovative Woman* magazine. In 2012, the El Camino College Foundation honored her as a Distinguished Alumni of the Year. She is also a member of the American Institute of Professional Bookkeepers and a 2012 Service Business of the Year finalist (also *Today's Innovative Woman*).

Lease Commercial Space with Ease

Set your business up for success, avoid these common pitfalls

By Heidi Hoch, Commercial Broker

Running a successful business means having access to the best Commercial Office, Retail or Warehouse space available. Often, however, even the most seasoned business owners run into a multitude of obstacles when trying to locate and secure Commercial Space that is suitable and affordable for their needs. From deciding what type of Commercial Space is best for business growth to negotiating the terms of a commercial lease, there are some guidelines that can help you take your business to the next level of success.

As an experienced Commercial Tenant Representation Broker (Tenant Rep. Broker) with more than 15 years in the industry, I have personally seen my share of the good, the bad and the ugly in the leasing of Commercial Real Estate. The truth is, there are many things that can go wrong without representation. On the flip side, there are also many things that can work in your favor when your representative finds you the right Commercial Space.

In this chapter, I am here to help you achieve your dreams with some expert guidance on how to select and negotiate the best commercial lease, and most importantly, share tips on how to avoid the common pitfalls in leasing Commercial Space.

Aim High on Your Wish List

Attaining a Commercial Space where your business will thrive first takes a dream. Consider the image of how you want your business to look. How do you want to spend your days? What are the types of clients with whom you will be working? This gives you the foundation of your wish list for finding the right place for your business. While there is no "perfect" Commercial Space, you want to aim high and start with the things you value the most.

For example, you may want to have an office with a unique atmosphere. Perhaps you have a tech company requiring primarily open office space. Maybe you want bike storage for the type of employees you hire. Perhaps you want ease of access to public transportation or maybe you want to include fun elements, such as slides between floors. For most business owners, some of the top values are monthly budget, upfront costs when signing the lease, size of space, demographics and location. Think about what you value the most and how your space can help your business flourish.

"Your mind can build castles—
just make sure the foundations are in place first."
—Donald Trump, American business magnate, investor,
television personality and author

Narrow your search for a Commercial Space by looking for these factors. Too many business owners start their search wide open, leading to unfavorable compromises and choosing the wrong location. It is a balancing act of being narrow enough, yet not too restrictive.

When making your wish list, consider your plans for the future growth of your business, as well as an appropriate location for the type of business you operate. For example, when looking at the location for your business, ask yourself, *Who is my target demographic for clientele? Where do my employees live and can they get to my newly leased Commercial Space easily in traffic or via public transportation?* These are some of the many questions that the right Commercial Space will answer.

Another factor to consider is the time you need to secure a space. For most businesses, expect the process to take between six and nine months. This is time you will need to locate, negotiate and secure the most appropriate Commercial Space. As you move ahead, evaluate your business start or re-launch date and watch out for new construction that could delay your business's grand opening. I have seen several businesses fail because the owners did not coordinate their business launch date with the actual completion of a newly constructed Commercial Space.

Also, I encourage you to err on the side of caution when it comes to construction of Tenant Improvements—TI's—in a leased commercial. Plan for thirty to ninety days for the TI's to be completed. Even the best of well-crafted leases by the greatest of real estate attorneys fall prey to unforeseen delays—this is because the lease document is always crafted prior to construction beginning.

Some of the tips I give my clients are simply common sense, yet often forgotten in the excitement of choosing a Commercial Space. Spend more time planning for your space than going out to look for it. Many business owners make the mistake of looking for space too soon, before they are aware of what their budgets are or where their business needs to be located. It is truly a waste of time to start looking for space before you have your plan in place. Get your house in order first! Start with your financials, budgets and space requirements.

Super Tip: A good Tenant Rep. Broker will help you get started on making sure your business house is in order before you tour your first property.

Try not to be shortsighted when it comes to your business location. Understand you have a budget and a growth plan for the business. As you begin to plan for this growth, think of Commercial Real Estate in terms of the beginning, the middle and the end. Go beyond the short-term needs and take a closer look at the potential long-term forecast of your business.

I always say, *Think with the end in mind,* which may sound a bit strange at first. However, what happens if your business expands over three to five years and suddenly you find yourself with an expired lease? What if there is no more room in your current building to expand, therefore requiring you to relocate your business?

A Commercial Real Estate Broker—more specifically a specialist such as a Tenant Rep. Broker—has the knowledge to guide you as a partner in your business growth. Partnering with an experienced Tenant Rep. Broker often gives you access to vendors who are experts on your side, such as architects, space planners, commercial insurance brokers, Commercial Real Estate attorneys and business attorneys. All of these professionals can help you plan for your business today and in the future. Having a Tenant Rep. Broker as a partner can give you peace of mind that wherever you are in the growth cycle of your business, you can truly have it all.

The Deal is Way Beyond Rent:
Focus on Negotiating Your Lease Terms

Perhaps one of the biggest mistakes a business owner can make is choosing to accept the terms of a Commercial Space, without considering the complete needs of the business or the terms of the lease. Often, what seems like a minor clause can have serious repercussions. With the help of an experienced Tenant Rep. Broker you can get the Commercial Space you need with terms that are more favorable to you. Try to think of all the ways your business will evolve over time and what the space can offer you before you sign on the dotted line.

Super Tip: Set yourself up for success before touring spaces. Plan ahead! What does your Commercial Space require? An elevator? Access to a kitchen or break room for staff? Giant lobby? A boardroom? What are the unique needs of your business as it relates to your space? Whatever those are, have your Tenant Rep. Broker target those spaces for you.

> *"Risk comes from not knowing what you're doing."*
> **—Warren Buffett, American business magnate,**
> **investor, philanthropist**

Here are some common lease clauses to negotiate for the future success your business:

- **Expansion option** is a right that typically stipulates the Landlord is obligated to provide the Tenant with more space, should the space be available and upon demand from Tenant.
- **Termination option** or buy-out option are both example clauses in a lease giving the Tenant the right to break the lease under certain conditions, such as when the Tenant needs to expand or vacate a Commercial Space.

- **Renewal option** gives the Tenant a right to remain in the premises upon expiration of the current lease term for a period of time. The rental rate is typically negotiated at the time of renewal.
- **Option to sublease** is a right, which gives the Tenant the option to sublease the space, thus offering some flexibility and cost savings if the business must relocate before the lease terminates.

A Tenant Rep. Broker will negotiate specifics as it relates to your lease once he or she fully understands the needs—present and future—of your business.

The true cost of the space you may be leasing for your business may be modified and discounted for various reasons. Landlord incentives and improvements made can help your business reduce these costs, particularly on a second-generation space. For example, you may decide to open a dental office in a Commercial Space that was previously used as a medical office or was a former dental office. This choice helps reduce the startup costs of building-out the space.

Rental fees, submitting financials and security deposits are other areas where I see business owners struggle time and again. Savvy business owners must understand that everything is negotiable, including lease terms, deposits and guarantees. It is extremely important for business owners to understand there are different rental rate types. To understand how to get the true monthly cost in order to compare spaces equitably please refer to the graph on page 17.

When faced with the demand for a security deposit or a personal guarantee, do you know how to respond? Your business credit-worthiness may negate the requirement for a hefty security deposit and you may be able to limit your personal guarantee on a lease. Rental fees can be discounted according to certain criteria, such as length of the lease term and any upgrades you make to the space. Are you aware of what you should disclose when submitting financials such as a business plan, profit and loss statements, bank letter of credit or line of credit?

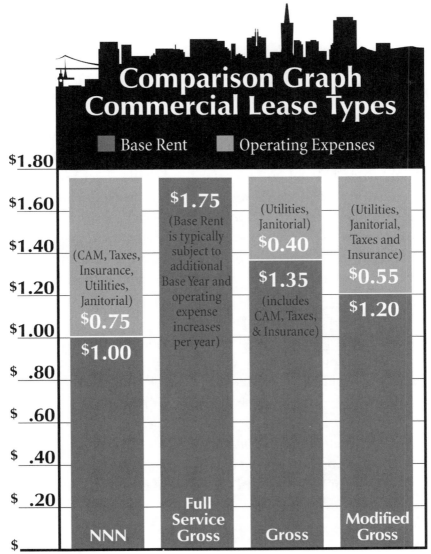

Comparison Graph
Commercial Lease Types

Base Rent   Operating Expenses

	NNN	Full Service Gross	Gross	Modified Gross
Operating Expenses	$0.75 (CAM, Taxes, Insurance, Utilities, Janitorial)		$0.40 (Utilities, Janitorial)	$0.55 (Utilities, Janitorial, Taxes and Insurance)
Base Rent	$1.00	$1.75 (Base Rent is typically subject to additional Base Year and operating expense increases per year)	$1.35 (includes CAM, Taxes, & Insurance)	$1.20

Disclaimer: Tenants should always ask what costs are included in your Base Rent and paid in addition to! Costs are not universal and differ from building to building. The above graph is based off general definitions of costs typically paid by Tenant under each Lease type. Landlords pass thru costs accordingly as they so choose subject to negotiation by Tenant, general accounting principles and the law.

Hire a Professional Who Represents You as the Tenant

As a business owner, you do have certain rights and responsibilities when obtaining Commercial Space. You have the responsibility to look out for you! You have the right to representation when leasing a Commercial Space.

The Landlord—an owner of a Commercial Space—has two goals: to get the most money from you and to get the lease terms in the favor of the Landlord. Therefore, the Landlord does not have your best interests in mind during this transaction. The Landlord has the right to representation in most cases. Specifically, he or she can hire a Listing Broker, who is a commercial broker representing the interests of the Landlord. Often, Landlords leverage the use of their Listing Broker—who appears to be concerned with your business's well being—when in fact that person is just trying to learn as much as he or she can about you to use it to the Landlord's advantage.

Look at it this way: It is highly unlikely you would ever go to court without an attorney, nor would you use the opposing side's counsel. Be a smart business owner and lease a Commercial Space with a Tenant Rep. Broker on your side. Level the playing field!

> *"It is true that you may fool all the people some of the time;*
> *you can even fool some of the people all the time;*
> *but you can't fool all of the people all the time."*
> **—Abraham Lincoln, 16th President of the United States**

When you work with a Tenant Rep. Broker, you partner with an advocate who can respond to intimidating Landlords and Listing Brokers to address difficult lease terms. Think of it this way: A Listing Broker is on the Landlord's team and is concerned only with the Landlord's interest and fiduciary duty. A Tenant Rep. Broker is on *your* team representing *your* interests. You would not walk into a basketball game expecting the other team's coach to look out for your best interests, would you? Get a "coach" who looks out for *you!*

Here is a typical scenario: You find a Commercial Space you would like to see and on your visit you meet a savvy Listing Broker. Walking through the place, you exclaim, "Wow, I really love this space!" If the Listing Broker hears you, the price just went up 10 percent or more. This emotional attachment will blind you to the fact that the Landlord and Listing Broker are already drawing up a contract that sticks you with the financial burdens of a Commercial Space that may not be good for your business. The Landlord and Listing Broker are "phishing" for information from you.

Super Tip: A wise businessperson once told me, "Listen more than you speak." Therefore, it is best not to say much on a market tour of Commercial Spaces for lease. Always have your Tenant Rep. Broker with you!

Tenant Rep. Brokers protect your business. Here are some of the benefits you receive when you work with an experienced Tenant Rep. Broker:

• There is no fee involved. It does not cost you money to hire a Tenant Rep. Broker. He or she can only save you money. The Landlord commonly pays a set fee to the Listing Broker. The Listing Broker keeps the entire fee if the Tenant does not have a Broker, or splits the fee with the Tenant's broker. Understand that the fee for both brokers in a lease transaction has already been factored into the deal.
• They can help reduce rent over the lease term and also negotiate free monthly rent.
• They can negotiate for the Landlord to pay for some, or in certain cases, all construction costs for TI's in your leased space.

- They can negotiate favorable lease terms such as expansion options, renewal options, termination options, purchase options and any other options that favor you, the Tenant.
- They can avoid or reduce causes and penalties for default by the Tenant wherever possible in a lease agreement, such as increasing the number of days in a contract.
- They can make sure the construction of improvements, property updates to your specifications and time specifications are provided in detail in the lease agreement.
- They can stop or limit future rental rate increases, hidden fees and out-of-control operating expenses.

> *"A good negotiator must be flexible to be successful.*
> *In a good negotiation, all sides win."*
> **—Donald Trump, American business magnate, investor,**
> **television personality and author**

Achieve your dreams with expert guidance on how to select and negotiate the best Commercial Space, and most importantly, how to avoid the common pitfalls in leasing Commercial Space by following these important guidelines:

1. Hire a Tenant Rep. Broker to protect your business interest.

2. Plan ahead. How much space do you need? Where is it located? What does the space plan and layout look like for your business? What is your budget?

3. Remember that no perfect space exists. You make the space become your reality.

4. Have your financial house in order prior to looking for space. I see this happen all too often with business owners. Financials can include profit and loss statements, your past two years of tax returns, your business plan, financial forecast and bank statements. I encourage you to speak with lenders, financial advisors and accountants, too.

5. Focus your requirements. It is a balancing act of being narrow enough, yet not too restrictive, either.

6. Be realistic about the market conditions, from expectations to rental rates to what you can expect the Landlord to address.

7. Everything is negotiable in Commercial Real Estate.

8. Listen more than you talk when speaking to a Landlord or a Listing Broker.

9. Ask questions! You can never ask enough questions when it comes to Commercial Real estate. Even if you know the answer, ask anyway. Sometimes you will learn more just by hearing the other person's response.

10. Think with the end in mind when leasing space. Often, I find a majority of costs and legal implications come to the Tenant's knowledge during and at the end of a lease term.

Choosing a Commercial Space for lease is an exciting time for your business. It can be a great learning experience, especially when you partner with a Tenant Rep. Broker to help you navigate the unfamiliar world of Commercial Real Estate. While some of the above pitfalls may concern you—and they should on some levels—you do not have to face them with uncertainty.

Remember, once more like a song bird singing in your ears, I encourage all business owners to hire a Tenant Rep. Broker to protect your business when leasing Commercial Space.

To learn more about how you can Lease Commercial Space with ease for your business, visit *www.heidihoch.com*. Sign in and receive your free copy of my lastest eBook, *Leasing Space with Ease: Top 10 Tips to Know Before You Start Leasing Commercial Space.*

Heidi Hoch

Commercial Broker

Finding Commercial Space With Ease

415-515-3295
heidi@heidihoch.com
www.heidihoch.com

Heidi Hoch, founder of Hoch Consulting, is a licensed Commercial Real Estate Broker specializing in Tenant Representation of leasing and buying Commercial Office, Retail and Warehouse Space. During her 15-year career, Heidi has been responsible for leasing and buying more than five million square feet of commercial space. Her expertise is in negotiations, financial controls and problem resolution, lease and landlord negotiations, acquisitions and dispositions. Her clients range from small businesses to private investors to multi-billion dollar international companies.

Since founding Hoch Consulting over five years ago, Heidi's most satisfying work is with smaller businesses and startups—setting her clients up for success and sustainability by finding and negotiating the perfect space for them. Add in her unique mix of advocacy and business savvy, and her reputation grows to include business owners who have tripled their revenue after consulting with Heidi.

Heidi was recently nominated for 2013 Northern California Real Estate Women of Influence award. She regularly speaks on several topics, most notably the "new normal" in Commercial Real Estate leasing. She has presented to the California State Bar, the San Francisco Lawyers Network and various other business associations throughout California.

Cultivating the Mindset of an Entrepreneur with Ease

By Mary Botham

Have you ever wondered if entrepreneurs think differently? Yes, they do, and the good news is that everyone can use the following seven techniques to cultivate the mindset of an entrepreneur. Mastering these techniques will give you greater ease in your business, allowing you to transform it into your "Blissne$$." I have acquired the mindset of an entrepreneur from being self-employed since 1979—and you can cultivate your mindset much quicker using these techniques.

First let me back up and tell you a little bit about my journey. In 1977, I graduated from the University of Colorado with a business degree and got married two months later. It was expected that those of us in the business school would go to work for big corporations. However, a friend wanted to know if we would be interested in starting a wholesale fish business in California. The friend was a fisherman and wanted someone with business knowledge.

I could tell you many stories about those early years. We were young and inexperienced, yet determined to make a go of the business. Our friend would catch the fish and my husband and I would sell them. At first we did not even know the names of the fish because we were landlubbers from Colorado. We worked out a system where he would memorize half the names of the fish and I would remember the other half. We would drive from Half Moon Bay to Chinatown in San Francisco to sell the fish in Asian markets.

Today, our business, Princeton Seafood Company, has grown into a full-service restaurant and fish market generating over seven figures annually.

In 2004, we realized that we had not planned for our retirement. Researching solutions, I came across the work of author Robert Kiyosaki and his Rich Dad Poor Dad series. The author explains that a small business owner trades hours for dollars the same way an employee does, and I saw clearly for the first time the predicament we were in. Our small business required our daily input for its success and yet our dream was to travel and not be at the restaurant every day. I became determined to become an investor and have our money create a cash flow that was not dependent on our day-to-day input.

I set a goal to purchase $1 million in investment real estate in appreciating markets over the next two years. I accomplished that goal and today we have nine homes in five states. Currently my husband and I are operating our restaurant and fish market as true business owners, rather than a mom and pop shop. Plus, I enjoy coaching women who want to grow a successful business.

The reason for our success has been because we developed an entrepreneurial mindset.

By definition, an entrepreneur organizes or operates a business often with a financial risk. When we first started our restaurant we borrowed $5,000, a huge sum at the time.

Entrepreneurs are often innovators—they create something new that was not there before. They see problems in the marketplace and develop solutions. Entrepreneurs respond to changes and capitalize on the opportunity and create a profit. Out of the profit, they pay themselves, they expand and they help others.

A mindset is a set of assumptions held by a person. To believe that you can cultivate your mindset requires a growth mindset. A growth mindset believes that you can constantly grow, improve and innovate. My father used to say, "Once you have it perfect, see what you can do to make it better." I used to hate hearing that when he was talking about my English papers, however I find it true in my life today. Business owners are constantly looking for ways to innovate and improve.

I have created an acronym around the word *mindset* to help you remember the steps and techniques to follow.

Cultivating and Improving Your M.I.N.D.S.E.T with Ease

M stands for motivation. Your motivation is developed because of your commitment to your dream. Galvanizing your motivation is like having magic! It works when you know where you want to go—your why. Being clear about your destination, your dream, even before you know everything about how to get there creates your inner motivation to achieve it. (See Joe Hunnicutt's chapter, *Igniting a Fire for What You Do,* on page 199)

My dream has always been financial freedom, where work is optional. I know that there are many paths to this dream. By setting an intention to move toward my dream, I am constantly looking to see that I am moving on a path toward my dream and not something else. Knowing what I am working for has become my motivation.

What is your why as an entrepreneur? Every day, remind yourself of where you are going and set an intention based on what you are willing do that day to move you toward your dream. Your intention will become your best time management tool. Intentional focus on your why gives you the motivation to work your business, especially during difficult times. With practice, your motivational muscle will become stronger and stronger.

I stands for internal rehearsal. As you become more and more clear about your dream, spend time imagining positive outcomes to your tasks. For example, in the restaurant business, I like to imagine opening the front doors as smiling families stream in and sit down. Our competent server takes their order and returns shortly with plates of delicious seafood. The customers ooh and aah over the presentation and the taste, and as they leave, tell me they cannot wait to tell their friends how much they enjoyed their meal. By imagining this scenario in my mind first, I can later create the results in reality. This internal rehearsal allows me to refine and define the steps necessary to create the results.

Athletes worldwide are using internal rehearsal with great success. Recently, I met an award-winning gymnast from Eastern Europe. When I asked her if she had ever used internal rehearsal, she looked at me with surprise and then told me that she had been part of a unique group. Half of the gymnasts were given an extra coach and the other half were not. This extra coach helped them mentally rehearse for several hours each Friday, going through their gymnastic routines in their mind, not on the mat. Once they were able to get their routines clear in their mind, their group consistently scored better than the group without internal rehearsal.

Think about how you want to improve your business and start mentally rehearsing your day as if you have already made the improvements. Perhaps you need to make some phone calls. Mentally rehearse going to the phone and imagine your prospect is on the other side waiting expectantly for you to call. She is excited and happy to talk to you and hear how you can help her. You clearly articulate what you want to say and you imagine yourself jumping up excitedly after the call because you just acquired a new client.

Our minds do not know if something is really happening or if we are only imagining it. You can activate positive emotions even if it is only happening in your mind. Thus, by using internal rehearsal, you can activate your positive emotions and develop action steps to create the business you want.

N stands for narrative. What are you telling yourself and others? Is it even true? Instead of a negative story, find the silver lining or positive aspect of your narrative. Review the lessons you learned. Often it is from hardship that we experience our biggest growth.

From 2004 to 2009, I created a portfolio of real estate at a purchase value of about $2 million. I had used the equity in our primary home as a down payment on an investment home and when that home increased in value I pulled out the equity and bought two more homes and repeated the process. Between 2009 and 2010, the values significantly dropped, some by half. I felt guilty that I created a financial meltdown for our family. The story I was telling myself was, *How could I be so stupid,* and *The equity in our home was supposed to be for our retirement and now it is gone!*

One day, I decided to change the narrative. I realized if I had not taken the equity out of our primary residence, we would have lost it anyway because the price of homes dropped nationwide. I also realized that if I could keep the investment homes, we would emerge from the financial crisis better than if I strategically defaulted as some financial experts advocated. I have been able to keep the majority of our homes and stabilize our finances because I changed my story. Today, with real estate rebounding, I know this was a good decision.

What is the narrative that you are telling yourself and others? How could you change it? If you had not experienced whatever hardship you went through, would you be the person you are today? What is the positive narrative of your life?

D stands for decisive action. The only way you can demonstrate to yourself that you are an entrepreneur is to take action on your business simply because it matters to you. That is the only way. Entrepreneurs have the mindset that they will take decisive action.

When I decided to buy real estate, I wrote the goal down on an index card and taped it to our bathroom mirror. Setting that goal was one of the hardest things I have ever done. Honestly, I was not sure how to put all the pieces in place and I knew it would require massive decisive action. I also knew I was willing to do whatever it would take to succeed.

As a coach, we call this creating a *WOW*. What action are you willing to do **W**ithin **O**ne **W**eek to move your business forward? What action are you willing to commit to for your business this week?

Taking decisive action requires a team because you will not have expertise in every area. If you are procrastinating, give yourself a deadline to complete the action. Ask someone to keep you accountable. Get the support you need so you can take decisive action.

S stands for self-care. The easiest way to give yourself self-care is to do something you love every day. As parents, we are naturally on the lookout for things our children enjoy and have an interest in. If they are interested in music, we sign them up for piano lessons. If they love horses, we enroll them in pony camp. You can do this for yourself. What did you like to do as a child that you could pursue now? Investigate ways you can have more of what you love in your life right now.

Take care of your body by eating nutritious food, exercising and getting enough sleep. Care for yourself with the same devotion that you would your child. Develop an attitude of gratitude for your talents and the work you are called to do.

Self-care is a necessary part of being successful and allows you to enjoy the fruits of your work. Sometimes it is the simple things that will best nurture you. Consider taking walks or enjoying a cup of tea while having a conversation with a friend. It might be scheduling an exotic vacation or getting your feet massaged. By nurturing yourself and doing what you love, you will appreciate your business more. Your mind will be more energetic and excited about the work you have chosen when you expand your self-care.

E stands for empowering beliefs. Many people are mean to themselves. If you are telling yourself that you are not good enough, not worthy or too overwhelmed, you are sabotaging your very success. Notice if you are complaining and critical all the time rather than building yourself up. Instead, you can encourage yourself with a new belief.

To create a new empowering belief, think about what attributes or values you would like to embody. Pick three values and fill in the blanks of this sentence:

*I am a _____, _____ and
_____ woman (or man).*

For example, "I am a trusting, courageous and wise woman" has been my empowering belief for several years. When I first chose this belief, those values were not how I would have described myself—now I have grown into the words.

Be diligent about looking in the mirror and confidently stating your new belief. Like the comic book hero Superman, stand with your shoulders back, hands on hips—it makes you feel more powerful and certain. As you are taking decisive action and working in your business, notice when you are stepping into your values and congratulate yourself. Keep encouraging yourself to step more fully into your new belief. Pick words that encompass your highest values.

As you begin to encourage yourself you will notice that not all of your friends are encouraging. You do not need crabby people pulling you down.

When the fishermen bring crab to our fish market, they bring them in uncovered crates. The crab on top of the heap could easily crawl out. However the moment that top crab starts to move, the crab on the bottom grabs hold, keeping the top crab pinned down. To move out of the box the pinned crab would have to sacrifice a leg. We do not need friends who are crabs. We need friends who are encouraging and celebrate our successes as we climb out of our box. More than anything, we need to encourage ourselves with an empowering belief.

T stands for transformation. The only thing certain is change. The process of transformation is seeking out, welcoming and leading change as part of personal growth. As entrepreneurs, we are called to transformation in three areas—personally, in our business and in the world.

In her book *Mindset* (Ballantine Books, December 2007) author Carol Dweck documents her research with children to determine if they developed a fixed mindset or a growth mindset depending on how they were praised. She cites many examples of children who were praised for talent, yet by the time they were in middle school, they did not try hard to do anything because their talent was not something they could control. These children developed a fixed mindset.

On the other hand, children who were praised when they were working hard or staying on task until mastery developed a growth mindset. These children learned to be excited when they were working hard because they knew they were completing a task or learning a new skill. Cultivating a growth mindset leads to positive transformation.

What are you doing on a daily basis to transform yourself? Evaluate what skills you need to learn to become the entrepreneur that you dream of being and decide to master that skill. Look honestly at where you are spending your time, energy and money. You can ensure your transformation by investing in yourself. Ask other successful entrepreneurs to describe what training or coaching helped them to transform themselves and invest similarly. Believe you are worth the investment.

At the end of your day, focus on where you worked hard, learned a new skill or completed something you committed to do. Praise yourself for a job well done and feel pleased that you did what you said you would do. As you intentionally notice your transformations, it will get easier and easier to move out of your comfort zone and into the new you that you are creating.

Decide where your business needs to transform. Hire the people who will facilitate the transformation you desire. Stay focused on the business that you want to create as a guide.

Your business provides transformation for others, even if you have not thought of it that way before. Know what the transformation is so that you can articulate it easily. Regularly collect testimonials to read to remind yourself and others of the transformation your business creates.

Transform the world by sharing your gifts and by giving back. Many spiritual practices teach the responsibility of tithing and also the joy that comes to the donor in even greater measure. Decide how you will give back and then take action to do so. Your philanthropy can transform the world.

Business success is really an inside job, happening first in the six inches between your ears. Using motivation, internal rehearsal, a positive narrative, decisive action, self-care, encouragement with an empowering belief and seeking transformation, you can cultivate your mindset to create Business Blissne$$ with ease.

Mary Botham
Mary Botham Consulting

650-868-2383
mary@marybotham.com
www.marybotham.com
www.princetonseafood.com

Mary is a sought after speaker with a warm style that is engaging and dynamic. The combination of connecting emotionally with audiences and delivering techniques that make immediate contributions to their bottom line stimulates transformation. Her energy is contagious whether speaking on entrepreneurship or life lessons as a Christian mother.

Using personal business acumen and proven methodologies as a Certified Dream Coach®, Mary inspires women to transform their business into their "Blissne$$." She is uniquely qualified to share her core message of "dream, decide and do."

In her role as a coach Mary encourages women to turn their dreams into dollars. She gives targeted, down to earth advice, practical tips and intuitive guidance. She can quickly guide a client to identify their unique gifts to bring solutions to the marketplace. Because she is a trusted expert in the fields of business ownership and real estate investing, her "Brilliant Brainstorming" and masterminds receive rave reviews.

Mary is passionate about art and has a dream to travel to one new country—or more—each year.

Visit www.marybotham.com to download *How to use a Simple 3x5 Card to Manifest Your Wildest Dreams.*

The Write It, See It, Say It to Achieve It™ Method to Achieving Your Goals with Ease

By Pam S. Russell

Do you set sales goals that you do not achieve? That was me many years ago. I am sure you have heard that goals must be Specific, Measurable, Attainable, Realistic and Timely (SMART). That is a great start, however in my world goal setting goes much deeper than that. I created the *Write It, See It, Say It to Achieve It* method. This process has helped me experience great success in achieving my goals.

Write It, See It, Say It to Achieve It is a four-step process where you first write down a goal, place an image of what represents that goal where you can see it every day and then say it out loud so it becomes a daily or hourly affirmation. You will be amazed how quickly you start to achieve your goals by following this method. I will explain how the process works in just a moment.

Prior to creating this method, I was constantly frustrated and disappointed because most of my goals would not come to fruition. I would write my annual sales goals down and then just blindly set out to try and accomplish them by the end of that year. Many times I felt like it was the blind leading the blind because most of my previous managers did not have a creative and precise way to teach me how to reach my goals either. Sadly, based on my experience, this seems to be the case in many companies, with most sales professionals and for the majority of entrepreneurs. At least you know you are not alone, right? Now let us dive in so I can teach you how to achieve your goals with ease.

Write It

Have you ever written your goal down in ink on paper so you can see it every day? If you answered *yes*—congratulations! You are way ahead of most other people and it is a great step in the right direction, or should I say write direction? If you answered no, do not feel bad. Most people cannot answer yes to that question. As you might have guessed, the first thing to do in my method is to write your goal down in ink on paper.

Next, determine what actions you need to prepare to accomplish each week, month and quarter to move you toward achieving that sales goal. A crucial part of that goal achievement equation is knowing your conversion ratio. "Conversion" in this case means knowing how many prospects you convert to paying clients. Track this number for a month or more. This generates the reliable data you need so you can break your goal down into manageable steps.

For example, let us say your goal is to generate $1 million in sales, with a conversion rate of ten to one. This means that every ten prospects you meet with results in one client. Research shows that on average it takes getting a *no* ten times before you get a *yes*. I usually keep track of every *no* I get so I know how close I am to getting a *yes*. It is a mind game that works for me, and it might work for you, too. I have a big YES on my *See It* board and say "I am getting lots of yeses!" out loud with confidence—like I mean it, baby!

As a reminder, if those no's are getting you down, remember that a no from a prospect or client does not always mean no forever. It might mean no for now.

Let's go back to the $1 million sales goal, and your conversion rate of ten to one. You have existing clients who bring in $600,000 a year for you. For this example we will say that your average client spends $50,000 a year with you. Based on your conversion ratio of ten to one, you will need to meet with eighty qualified prospects over the year and convert eight of them to new clients ($400,000) to meet your goal. You could be even more precise and plan to convert two prospects a quarter so that by year-end, you will have the eight new clients—two new clients times four quarters equals eight new clients—you planned for at the beginning of the year.

This is an oversimplified example. When working with my clients, we dig in much deeper to develop an even more precise plan to hit the conversion target. We consider other data and tactics required to meet their goals. In this way, we create a plan that helps my clients—and now you—achieve your sales goals.

I encourage you to look at your goals every day—multiple times a day is even better. Put them on your bathroom mirror. Put them in your wallet. Make them your screen saver on your computer. Write them on flash cards. Make reviewing your goals a part of your daily routine.

See It

The See It element is one of my favorite parts of this process. I believe it is important to visualize, to see, what you want to achieve. Seeing your goals every day—even multiple times a day—helps set your conscious and unconscious mind on them. It helps your brain keep them top of mind. Your brain is a powerful machine that processes an astronomical number of images, feelings, senses and information every day. We must remind it of what we want it to help us achieve, or it will focus on other things. We can do that by "seeing" our goals every day.

How do you add *See It* to your process? First you will need to make or buy a board to put your goals on. Most craft stores have pre-made corkboards that you can purchase. They often have them in beautiful frames that can actually be part of your office décor. It does not have to be expensive to work. Buy what you can afford. I have seen framed corkboards for as little as $10 at my local grocery store. I have a client who actually had corkboard installed on one entire wall in her office. Now that is thinking big!

Next, grab your list of goals. Let's use the example from the *Write It* section. You have set a sales goal of $1 million for the year. The first thing I would do is go online and find an image of a $1 million dollar bill, print it, cut it out and stick it on the board using pushpins. Using pushpins makes it easy for you to update your *See It* board regularly. You could even write the number in black marker on a piece of paper and put it on your board. It does not have to be complicated. Pull out all those old magazines you have stacked in the closet, thumb through them and get to cutting. You can even cut out words that are inspiring to you and put them on your board. It is that simple. If you have set a goal to go to Hawaii on vacation, go online to find an image of the specific resort where you want to stay, activities you want to do and what kind of rental car you want to drive. Put all of that on your *See It* board.

Keep in mind that the images on your *See It* board must align with your written goals. You can also add encouraging and inspiring words, just make sure that all of your written goals are represented by images on your *See It* board.

Here is a good example of how "seeing" your goals on a regular basis can help you succeed. In the 1980 World Series, Tug McGraw, former Philadelphia Phillies pitcher and father of country singer Tim McGraw, struck out Willie Wilson in a play that clinched the title for the Phillies. When asked how it felt to pitch the winning strike, McGraw explained that as a young child he would pitch to his dad in their backyard. He would envision that it was the bottom of the ninth inning and the count was two outs with three men on base in the World Series. He would get laser focused, pitch that ball to his dad and it would be a strike! So it came as no surprise that this exact scenario played out during the game—he had already played it out in his mind hundreds of times over the years. This is not only a great example of what seeing your goals can do for you; it is also a great example of visualizing a specific goal. McGraw did not just envision winning the World Series; he envisioned that it was the bottom of the ninth inning, with two outs and three runners on base. "See" what I mean?

Throughout his baseball career, McGraw encouraged Little League baseball players to practice autographing baseballs. What do you need to practice doing?

Another fun part of the *See It* process is putting the images of all the goals you have achieved in a binder. Think of it as your ongoing success story—it feels great to flip through the binder when you might be feeling discouraged or unmotivated to keep pushing toward your current goals. You can see all the wonderful things you have already accomplished. I recommend reviewing your *See It* board once a quarter. For the goals you have achieved, remove those pictures from the board and place them in your achievement binder. I tape or glue my achievement binder pictures to sheets of paper and then slide them into a protective clear view sleeve for easy viewing later on. You can buy the clear view sleeves at most office supply stores.

Say It

This is the second favorite part of my method. I believe you have to say your goals and desires out loud and with confidence—say it like you mean it, baby! This helps manifest them in your life. This is yet another way to set your mind on them. Some people think I am crazy for doing this—especially people in cars next to mine when they see me talking to myself at a stoplight. That is fine, I believe *Say It* works and therefore I do it. I know it sounds crazy and you might be thinking, *There is no way I am going to say my goals out loud.*

I am here to tell you that crazy has never felt as good as when the goals you have been saying out loud—after first writing them down and then placing them on your See It board—come to fruition.

Do you want to know what I say? Going back to our original $1 million example, here are a few suggestions.

When I put my makeup on in the morning I might say out loud and with confidence: *I am so proud of myself for selling $1 million this year. The feeling of accomplishment I have by achieving my goal is very rewarding.*

In your car on your way to a meeting you might say: *I am honored to be the featured speaker at the national conference for (say company name).* Or, *I am so grateful that my expert status got me booked as a keynote speaker at (say organization's name) annual sales meeting.*

You could even say, *I am excited to cash the $50,000 check I will get for giving a speech at the national conference for (say organization's name).*

Remember to say these words out loud and with confidence. Be as specific as possible. If your goal involves a specific company, person, place or thing, be sure to include that when you *Say It*.

Just a reminder, I have also written these goals down first in ink on paper. Where appropriate, I have put the company's logo—where I want to speak, who I want to do business with—on my *See It* board. I will often look at their logo on my *See It* board while I am saying the above statements. Then your brain *really gets it!*

Achieve It

Now that you are achieving your goals, what comes next? You reward yourself for all your hard work, perseverance and the great accomplishments you should be very proud of. Most of the time, I predetermine what my reward will be for each goal I set. The reward can be whatever you would like it to be. I try to make the reward match the effort it takes to achieve the goal. For example, when I achieve my $1 million sales goal I will reward myself with a week away at a fabulous beachside resort. I will put images of that resort on my *See It* board so that my goals are all in alignment. Then I would say something like, *I love swimming in the pool at (say resort name).*

Conclusion

This explains my *Write It, See It, Say It to Achieve It* method. It is an easy, unique and even fun process to achieve your goals and dreams.

If you follow this, I am confident you will begin to achieve great things in your life and business with ease. Now, I need to add one thing to my list of Its: *Try It,* you will like it.

> *"You will get all you want in life*
> *if you help enough other people*
> *get what they want."*
> **—Zig Ziglar, American motivational speaker**

One of my goals is to help as many people as I can achieve their goals—no matter how big or how small that goal might be. Through my coaching and speaking, I hope I have inspired many to think big and think a little differently about how to achieve their goals. When you help other people get what they want you will be richly rewarded for it. It may not necessarily be a monetary reward; however there are many things money cannot buy. I encourage you to do the same. Share the blessings of your success with others. It is quite possibly the easiest goal you will ever achieve!

For a free report on creative ways to get noticed by prospects that do not involve email marketing and auto-responders, please go to www.pam-russell.com/prospectingideas

Pam S. Russell

Sales Transformation Strategist, Speaker and Coach

Print and Promotions Expert

469-939-1678
pam@pamrussell.com
www.pamrussell.com

Pam Russell is a charismatic dynamo with an infectious personality. She is passionate about the sales process, setting goals and inspiring others to achieve sales excellence so they stop feeling frustrated and start being successful. She started her business in 2006.

Pam's clients include entrepreneurs, sales professionals and teams, direct marketers, speakers and coaches. Together, they create a sales blueprint that includes drilling down sales goals into a precise plan for achievement and developing a prospecting plan that gets results. She also helps clients determine who is—and is not—their ideal profitable client. Pam teaches clients how to create revenue streams from their expertise so that what seems like a lofty, sky-high sales goal becomes reality.

Pam's sales awards include Largest Single Order, Highest Average Order Size, Most New Clients and Most New Orders from Existing Clients in 30 Days, Centurion Award ($100,000+ sales increase in one year) and the Silver Award for Sales Excellence.

Pam is a native Texan who lives in Dallas. She owns Proforma Specialty Marketing—a printing and promotional product company. She is a single mom, dog lover, entrepreneur and speaker who appreciates a good sense of humor.

Trust Your Instincts for Successful Outcomes with Ease

By Carmen Okabe

Trust *your instincts.* You have heard that so many times before that you wonder, what is going to be said differently in this chapter?

Most likely, nothing new: all the words have already been said in this world, I will just tell you how listening to my instincts has worked for me.

I used to be the owner of a business a lot of people envied and many young ladies were attracted to work with me. Without being "the Devil wearing Prada," for nine years, I was the publisher of an international beauty magazine—with all the apparent advantages of that position.

Now I have come to believe that this was not meant to be on my life path, and all my achievements in that position—more than just a few—were obtained with a lot of difficulty because of this.

During those nine years, besides paying their salaries, I paid for the studies of many young ladies. I was their coach. I helped change their life path. I showed them how to live a healthier lifestyle and I gave them the taste for doing things which are making a difference today.

I helped the highest majority become beautiful women free of emotional complexes. When I first met them, some were fighting with acne, some were overweight, some did not consider themselves worthy of being loved and allowed their husbands or boyfriends to abuse them.

I helped many other women build their own businesses in the beauty sector. I helped them open beauty centers and nail spas. Some even became famous hairstylists. Sometimes I taught them how to simply make good decisions so they married a man who treated them well, instead of one who did not.

I also helped men start up viable businesses and regularly gave away, for free, companies and business ideas to people I cared about. Sometimes these decisions, these choices, were the wrong ones for me to make.

Why I am telling you this? To help you understand that, at all moments, I knew who could become my Judah: I knew who was stealing from me, who was cheating on me, who wanted to be me. Still, I chose to ignore my instincts and went ahead, investing in these people, with the hope my instincts were wrong.

Life has since proven me wrong and my instincts right. Life also proved I was not supposed to spend so much time and money for that business, it was a highly paid lesson I had to learn.

Now what I want to tell you is this: you can do whatever you want. If it is in your life's mission to do it, then it will be done with ease. If you go against the current and against your instincts, life will bring you tough moments, to say the least.

How many people do you know who studied so hard for so many long years in a field, yet failed to be successful? Others, however, met the right person at the right time and hit on the right idea and are now wildly successful.

I bet you can name at least a dozen, maybe yourself included.

"Follow your instincts. That's where true wisdom manifests itself."
—Oprah Winfrey, American media proprietor, talk show host, actress, producer and philanthropist

Our life path is the result of our choices. Be it at your work place, in school or at home, it is all about making decisions. Every step we initiate is the result of a decision. These decisions can be based on either reasoning or intuition.

Some would define intuition as a gut feeling, an instinct, a hunch or an inner knowing. It is most commonly known as "the inner voice." We generally try to listen to our inner voice in personal life, however do we listen to our inner voice when we talk about money? Maybe it is a decision involving a million-dollar contract, recognizing a business opportunity, hiring a skilled candidate or simply making a sales call at the right time. How accurate are one's decisions based on her instincts? Should we only use intuition and instinct to make business decisions or should it be combined with reason?

The Inspiration

When I decided to be part of this project, what came to my mind was the topic of instinct. What is instinct? That first impulse, the first thing your body pushes you to do—this is instinct. Then, of course you may choose to follow it with your mind or not.

Be sincere with yourself, as I am now, revisiting the many times I made decisions based on being rational: calculating, carefully planning those matters which, instinctively, I had felt signs I should *not do*.

Throughout the years of my career, I was confronted with daily business choices. My life has changed based on those decisions, which most of the time involved an emotional charge—a primary instinct.

For example, soon after the USSR divided into small republics, we were shopping wholesale for tons of caviar in the Caspian Sea region. We received an offer to buy caviar from official sources at the price of $20 per kilogram. The minister in charge was not aware that the international price was ten times higher at the time. They were still making a profit with their price; therefore I could have ethically just accepted the offer and added a few million dollars to my pocket.

Still, my instinct made me choose to thank him for the generous offer and brief him about all the international caviar regulations and price points. He was so surprised by my integrity that he took me straight to the president of the new republic and introduced me as the "business lady who did not try to cheat us." The president was so pleased that he appointed me as a consultant for the government's economic matters.

Over the next few years, I earned much more business and money than I would have made if I had chosen to buy the caviar at the original asking price and kept quiet. Until then, I believed that one's instinct for successful business comes from his or her own experiences. I had great role models around, very successful business people whom I admired for their achievements. I studied their way of doing business and tried to understand their decision-making style. I had neither their experience, nor their money to risk; yet my instincts helped me make decisions that brought me huge satisfaction.

In personal life or in business, whenever I listened to my instinct, the outcome was all right. Whenever I did not, the result would make me lose money, lose trust in people, lose time and so much more.

Trusting one's instinct is not a new concept in the business world. In fact, successful business leaders have a strong belief in their own intuition. For some leaders it is more accurate and reliable than any other resource they have for making decisions.

> *"Have the courage to follow your heart and intuition.*
> *Everything else is secondary."*
> **—Steve Jobs, American founder of Apple®**

Why You Should Trust Your Instinct

Have you ever feared someone you just met, without apparent reason? With no clear argument, you could not explain why you did not trust this person.

It is scientifically proven that our bodies react differently to people's energy, that the animal in us receives the signal to be wary, for her own survival. Yet most of the time, our inner voice argues with us and we want to be "in control." Therefore we ignore that inner voice, we ignore our fears. The human mind is a mysterious and powerful phenomenon that can do wondrous things even science fails to explain. According to science, people's instincts are manifestations of the unconscious mind.

Your unconscious mind captures and processes a lot of information from what you read, learn and experience, even from things you do not pay any attention to. Science has proven that our intuition, enriched by all this information, becomes a powerful and accurate tool in decision-making, ninety percent of the time.

Trusting your instinct has great advantages. You are the only one to be congratulated in case of success and you cannot blame anybody else in case of failure. This last is really relieving—how many times have you gotten angry because someone else made a mistake?

When to Use Your Instincts in Business

Here are some situations when instincts help you make better decisions.

- When **time sensitive** situations leave you no time to go through a complete rational analysis.
- When there is **insufficient data** and no way or time **to collect data** in order to analyze the situation
- When you have **ambiguous and conflicting information**.
- When there are **too many conflicting interests** arising from influential parties.
- When the **factors** to be taken into consideration **are changing rapidly**.
- When there are **too many factors, considerations and rules** you have to take into account that make it hard to have a clear vision.
- When the **problem is not clear** or is poorly identified.
- When **you are initiating** something which no one has done before. This means there are no predefined guidelines, standards, practice, models or patterns to follow.
- In **life-changing decisions**, those involving marriage, separations or moving from one country to another.

How Can You Empower Yourself to Trust Your Intuition?

When you have doubts, you may find it difficult to trust your instincts. Here are some ideas on how you can empower yourself to trust your instincts.

Listen to your inner voice and look for signs. Calm your mind, get free from negative emotions. Take a deep breath and focus on what is going on. Look around for signs that support your intuition. The answer can be in the title of a book you saw in a bookstore you just passed by, it could be in the phone call you received exactly when you had decided to quit if the phone did not ring. A sign is anything that is strong enough in that moment to make you listen to your instinct—and make that decision.

Question yourself, try meditation. If you are not satisfied with the ideas given by your intuition and still have doubts, hold a conversation between yourself and your intuition. Your memory has stored lots of information that you are unaware of, and if you really question your mind it will give you the reasons it came to this conclusion. Talking to your unconscious mind can be more effective by practicing meditation.

Do not lie to yourself. No matter what you have done, take the time to reflect on the experience. To what extent did you listen to your inner voice? What kept you from trusting your instinct? Be sincere with yourself about what your instinct told you to do, and what you chose to do instead.

Cross check with an astrologer or a Feng Shui practitioner about the place and the interaction between the energy of the people involved. I learned from my own experience that pushing against destiny or making decisions at the wrong time with the wrong people can cost you a lot. If you have the time, consider seeing a specialist. She will confirm your good instincts or will ask you to think twice before acting—the decision is still yours.

How to Use Your Instinct Effectively

It is true that intuition helps you navigate through unstructured data. It also generates the ability to evaluate certain gaps when you review conflicting information. Yet, intuition can be misled if the data collected by your unconscious mind and the facts you have collected are wrong or misleading. That means there is still a slight risk of making wrong decisions.

Therefore, to use your intuition effectively, please pay attention to your own emotional state. If you are mentally stressed during a situation or feel nervous, your intuition will be inaccurate, distracted by your strong negative feelings or thoughts. If you want your instinct to be effective and accurate, get free from your strong feelings by letting them go. You can take a walk, get refreshed, meditate or do anything that calms your mind.

Six Ways to Trust Your Instinct and Make Business Decisions with Ease

1. Follow your instincts and fully commit. When you let yourself be guided by your gut, passion follows. The instinct leads you to your motivation and work ethic. You are more likely to be right and feel encouraged to work hard in order to earn success. Have faith and live in the moment, be focused and do your best.

2. Make yourself go deeper into the idea. If you have serious doubts about your instincts in certain situations, do not ignore these signals. It is better to find all the insights and gather more information. This way you collect enough reasons to make a decision with confidence.

3. Do not be afraid to think outside the box. If it is something you are doing for the first time, do not be afraid to accept your instincts. Your creative mind knows what your abilities are. This is when your instinct tells you to go the unconventional path. You will find your way to win the challenge.

4. Ignore the conventions or rules. If your instinct tells you, this is not the way it should be done, it should be done differently, do not be afraid to challenge existing conventions or rules. Those were made by someone else's instincts five or fifty years ago, therefore think how things have changed over time! Now you may be the one to set new rules that solve tomorrow's problems.

5. Allow your idea to change or grow. When acting on your instinct, be flexible about the implementation. The basic instinct will stay the same, yet the idea will change and evolve.

6. Do not be afraid to take the risk. Listening to your inner voice in making business decisions may appear challenging and risky. If you trust your gut, then do not be afraid to take the risk. Risk and trust you will achieve your goals.

Trust Your Gut and Make the Right Choice for Success with Ease

In life or in business, learn to listen to your instincts. If you do not trust your gut, you will find yourself at odds. Train yourself to use your instincts effectively. Question yourself when you have doubts about your instincts. The answers to your problems lie within you.

You just have to find that little voice inside your mind that will give you the answers in any difficult situation.

Remember your mind is a powerful thing—it always guides you to the light. Find your own unique way in which your instinct talks to you. Making the right choices will lead you to have a successful life and business career. Trust your gut and take the challenge, take the risk and work for the outcome! You will find your own success with ease.

Carmen Okabe
Swiss Image Institute

+41 798 39 39 81
carmen.okabe@bluewin.ch
www.carmenokabe.ch

Carmen Okabe was born in Romania to parents of Turkish and Hungarian ancestry. She studied in China, married and lived in Japan, then further lived in France, Turkey, China, Belgium and Romania. Now based in Switzerland, Carmen runs The Swiss Image Institute and the Swiss Institute for Natural Medicines.

With diplomas in Oriental languages and in Japanese management, Carmen is a member of AICI, former vice president of education for the AICI France Chapter, and the founder and past-president of the National Union of Professional Beauticians in Romania. She published the professional beauty magazine Les Nouvelles Esthétiques for nine years and created Romanian-based Estetik TV, a channel dedicated to the world of image.

Carmen is a Licensed Mind Mapping Instructor, Executive Coach, Fashion Fengshui Facilitator, speaker and author with more than fifteen years of experience in the beauty and image industry. She speaks eight languages fluently: Chinese, Japanese, Turkish, English, French, Italian, Spanish and Romanian. Carmen offers classes on image transformation, personal development, Feng Shui for fashion, beauty and health and acts as a business consultant all over the world.

Contact Carmen at www.carmenokabe.ch to receive your free gift.

Customer Service IS the New Marketing

Create raving fans with the Nine Rules of customer service with ease

By Patrick H. Ennis

"You know, if you make a customer unhappy
they won't tell five friends, they'll tell 5,000 friends."
—Jeff Bezos, American CEO of Amazon.com

Studies show that people are three times more likely to believe a total stranger on social media than they will believe your company's advertising. What would it mean to your business if prospects sought you out, instead of you spending huge amounts of money on promotion efforts with low returns? Just turn your customers into raving fans, and they will tell everyone they know about how fantastic your business is! That is why customer service is the new marketing.

I spent more than 25 years working for Fortune 500 companies. I was always amazed at the emphasis we put on getting new business, and how little we put on keeping existing customers. Existing customers keep your business running and pay your bills, why would you ignore them and treat them with less respect than prospects? As a small business, you have an advantage because you can make sure you put as much effort into keeping your customer as you do into getting new ones.

In my role now as a marketing and business coach, I ask struggling clients, *When was the last time you talked to all your clients?* and *What kind of customer feedback mechanisms do you have?* Finally, *Do you have a program to regularly thank them for their business?* I'm usually met with silence as they realize that customer service is a lot more than just delivering a product or solution. That is why I developed my Nine Rules of customer service. These are easy for any business to put into action and will quickly turn your existing customers into evangelists who do your promotion for you. Here is how to get started.

Rule Number One: It Starts with a Promise—Deliver it

Are you Nordstrom® or Wal-Mart®? Both these companies are excellent at customer service in very different ways. When we walk in the door we do not expect to get Nordstrom service in a Wal-Mart. Vice versa, we do not expect to pay Wal-Mart prices in a Nordstrom either. Each company promises a type of service and then delivers it. Rarely do you leave without feeling you got what you came for. What is your promise, written and unwritten, to your clients? Do not promise they can return something anytime, if anytime is only for the first 15 days.

A few years ago, I hired a contractor to fix a 15-foot crack in my foundation wall. I explained my budget and what I could afford. When I got the bill, it was more than twice the agreed upon total! Needless to say, I was not happy. He said there was hidden damage and pointed out my contract was to pay by the foot. I will never know what really had to be fixed, and more importantly he knew my budget and had broken his promise. To this day, I tell anyone who asks never to do business with him.

This example shows that I hate surprises, therefore in my business we always point out the shipping, tax and other potential additional costs in our proposals. My promise is that you will not be surprised. Before I exceed the original projection I always notify the client. I lose lots of work to competitors who do not spell everything out because I appear to be more expensive on the surface, however I sleep nights and I have loyal, repeat customers. I know my values and I deliver what my customers expect.

Rule Number Two: Great Customer Service Starts with Having Great Customers

One of the best things about owning your own business is that you get to decide who you want to do business with. On the occasions when I fail to make a customer happy it is because I broke this rule. Occasionally, we take on a client who does not fit our expertise, is too small or too big for us, or has too tight a delivery window. Sometimes a client demonstrates pre-sale that they are difficult to work with, yet we ignore the warning signs. In the end, we deliver what we promised; however these kinds of clients take up an exorbitant amount of time and are not profitable. Meantime, our good clients suffer.

Recognize when a customer is putting you in a position to fail. Even if you are 100 percent in the right, at the end of the day, they will not see it that way and you will be the one who did not deliver. Good clients are the ones who understand that when they ask for something extra, you will have to charge for it. Bad clients are in it for them to win and you to lose, and that is not why you are in business.

Make a list of all your clients. Rank them by profitability. Then rank them again by return on investment (ROI). Even if you do not have hard numbers, do this step based on your gut feeling about them. Most likely your least profitable customers will be at the bottom of each list. It might be time to move them on—do not tell them you do not want their business, just raise your prices so they go somewhere else.

Rule Number Three: Whoever is Easiest to do Business with, Wins!

> *"Make your product easier to buy than your competition, or you will find your customers buying from them, not you."*
> **—Mark Cuban, American owner of the Dallas Mavericks**

Consider Blockbuster® and Borders®. These were good businesses, however tapes and paperback books were no match for "on-line streaming." Are you making it easy for your customer to do business with you? Time, honesty, service, guarantees and hours of operation are as important, or more so, than price to today's stressed buyer. This is not about technology or cost, it is about ease. The corner gas station can charge three times as much as the grocery store for a soda because when you are hot and thirsty they are right there and easier to do business with. Same soda, just faster and more convenient.

Great customer service starts with that first interaction, and that is most likely on your website. This is the first place they usually seek information. What does you website say about how easy it is to do business with you? Can prospects quickly find answers to their questions? Do they feel confident about choosing you? Is your website easy to read on a mobile device? Do you give them a way to take action immediately while still on your site? If you are making them call you, or send an email to get started, then you are not easy to do business with.

On the other end of the transaction, take a look at your invoice. Every time a client looks at your invoice they are going to make a decision about how satisfied they are with your service. Your invoice has to be easy to understand. This is especially true when you have multiple line items. Your invoice may be the last impression your client has until the next time your services are needed. Your invoice is an opportunity to demonstrate that you care about your buyer and that you listen. Ask yourself:

- Do the terms match the offer? Your invoice should match the offer exactly. Are the amounts and units of measure the same?
- Is your customer reminded of the value of your services? Do not just list *For Professional Services,* make a list of the main components you provided for that price.
- Are you making your buyer look good? Will your client have to explain to his or her boss why the invoice is different from the estimate?
- Can the accounting department pay the bill? Accounting departments can be big "influencers." If you know a packing slip or other paperwork is required, have you provided it? If your invoicing process is too complex or hard to understand, your buyer might decide it is easier to go to someone else.

Put yourself in your customer's shoes. If you were buying your product or service, what would you want? What would make it easier? Then make it happen.

Rule Number Four: Always Say *Yes!*

Customers expect a business to listen to and accommodate special requests. We all have had clients who called at a late date and asked to move up their schedule or change a specification. They ask because they need your help to make them successful. You would not be a good partner if you said *No*. Make sure your answer is always either *Yes* or *Yes, but*. Your job is to explain their options. It is not always easy, however this is the essence of customer service—getting the job done and making your customer look like a hero.

I have found that *Yes, but* has a formula:
• Yes, but...there is another way
• Yes, but...do you understand what else will be affected
• Yes, but...there is additional cost

Most big companies actually train their employees to say *No!* Instead, give your employees approval to say *Yes* and tell them they must get approval to say *No*. Customer satisfaction and finding a way is the primary job. Coach your employees to verify that a request can be accommodated, and then to document and get approval for extra costs.

Is there ever a right time to say *No?*
Yes, during the sale and solution development process. Some projects are too expensive, out of your area of expertise, bad for the customer and most importantly, potentially set you up for failure. Customers expect you to tell them if they are making a mistake. They will respect you more, even if it means you are losing a sale. Tell your customer *No* up front so you ensure delivery on your promises later.

Rule Number Five: Service Your Customer's Customer

"Quality in a service or product is not what you put into it.
It is what the client or customer gets out of it."
—Peter Drucker, Austrian-born American
renowned business consultant and author

If you want truly loyal fans, you have to help them achieve their goals. A customer does not buy a toaster, he buys the toasted bread. Be a partner in your customer's business. Train your employees to understand that client service is their fundamental job and you will have repeat customers.

Rule Number Six: Handle Complaints, Quickly

Unhappy customers cannot be avoided. It is important to handle them quickly and with genuine caring for their well being.

Timeliness Matters
Studies show that when a problem is responded to in a few hours, customer satisfaction goes up! If you wait 24 hours or more, satisfaction goes down, even when the problem was 100 percent resolved. It is crucial to respond quickly and fully to a customer complaint even when you cannot resolve the issue. Customers appreciate being told about setbacks so they can make other arrangements to achieve their goals.

Complaints become more expensive the longer you wait. Before you respond, or as you formulate your response, do a quick ROI analysis: What is keeping the customer worth to you? What is avoiding a bad review worth to you? Most importantly, what is having the problem hanging over you doing to the rest of your business? It is less expensive in the long run to resolve problems quickly.

How to Deliver Bad News

There is a formula for communicating bad news that maintains your customer's goodwill and heads off bad reviews. First decide if you will:

- Admit your mistake and correct the problem
- Recognize someone else's error, and correct the problem anyway
- Not admit fault, not take responsibility for fixing the problem

I often counsel my clients to check their ego at the door when they reach this stage. Nobody likes to admit they were wrong or are being taken advantage of, but emotion often gets in the way. Skip the history and focus squarely on the solution. What customers want more than anything is to know that you care. To make sure this happens, use this six-step process and pay particular attention to the order in which you communicate.

1. In response to the issue, what action you have taken?

2. Demonstrate you have investigated, include a short explanation of how the problem occurred.

3. Show your concern, apologize (if you are at fault) and be empathetic.

4. List steps you are taking to make sure it does not happen again.

5. Tell the customer you value their business and goodwill.

6. Change the subject.

Follow these steps—do not skip any—and you will be amazed how most situations can be diffused and actually create increased loyalty.

Rule Number Seven: Protect Your Online Reputation

The last thing you want is for a negative comment to go viral without any response from you. Here are some steps you must take to protect your on-line reputation:

- Sign up for Google® Alerts and similar services to be notified if your name, your business or your competitors are mentioned on-line.
- Dedicate someone to respond to issues and even compliments. They must respond in near real-time.
- Create a release valve—use feedback mechanisms such as response cards so people can register their concerns directly with you. Make sure you respond to indicate that you are listening.

A restaurant client of ours implemented a system so customers could use their smartphones to comment directly to management while they were still at the restaurant. Now management can address issues before they were shared on-line. Guess what? They have doubled membership in their loyalty club and they get tons of social media "shares." This approach turned unhappy customers into fans.

Rule Number Eight: Learn From Your Customers After the Delivery

Why do businesses ask you to rate your experience on a scale of one to ten? Marketers use your responses to create powerful analytics that tell them how they are doing in creating satisfied customers. You can implement satisfaction surveys with inexpensive tools like Survey Monkey® and Constant Contact®. Here's how a typical calculation works.

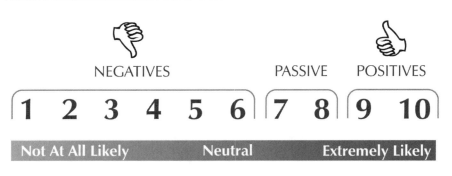

Score = Percentage of Positives **Minus** the Percentage of Negatives

Focus less on what your score is today. Instead, focus on doing the survey each time you make changes to your customer service process. This way you can measure if you are creating more or fewer satisfied customers.

Here are some simple changes you can make right away to raise your score:

• Create an email newsletter and social media program.
• Have a personal contact with every customer at least once a quarter to acknowledge them.
• Install an after sale *thank you* program, for example a card, a gift or a coupon.
• Capture all business activity in a central customer relationship management system such as SalesForce®.com or Insightly®.

When you follow up with your customers, pay special attention to your top accounts and, in particular, with the decision-makers if you sell complex programs. After a sale is made, it becomes easy to lose touch as your staff deals with their staff. However, the contract will need to be renewed, and you need referrals. Find ways to continue the conversation over a meal or a meeting.

Rule Number Nine: Always Remember the Lifetime Value

If repeat business is the goal, how come businesses do not do a better job with customer service? I find there are two main reasons. The first is fear, nobody wants to be judged or challenged and sometimes the truth hurts. The second is money. Responding and fixing problems costs money that usually is not in the job pro forma. I encourage my clients to always look at the long term "lifetime value" of relationship. By stepping back and realizing how much a customer is worth over the long term and through referrals, the problem becomes less personal and cost becomes less significant.

Conclusion

> *"Do what you do so well that they will want to see it*
> *again and again and bring their friends."*
> **—Walt Disney, American founder of Disneyland®**

Customer service is an attitude that starts at the top. Here are some changes you can implement right away to create raving fans.

1. Deliver service with a smile. Customers respond to cheerful employees. Add programs to make them happy. If you are a solo entrepreneur, find a seminar that refocuses you and motivates you to say *yes* more often.

2. Under-promise and over-deliver. Do your homework and deliver proposals with integrity. Will your customer be satisfied by your proposal, and will the invoice match the estimate?

3. Regularly review your customers, their profitability, and if they are a fit for your operation.

4. List your top customers, and call them every quarter just to say *Hi, how is it going?* Have a marketing plan for existing clients to remind them you appreciate them.

5. Conduct a customer service survey. Do not be defensive when you get the results, use them as a benchmark for improvement.

Follow these Nine Rules and you will be amazed by how easily you generate word of mouth advertising—and all the new customers and clients who come your way.

Patrick H. Ennis
Inc Marketing Services LLC
Impressive Results Start by
Making a Great Impression!

703-753-3733
pat@incmarketingservices.com
www.incmarketingservices.com

At the request of a small business client who needed marketing support, in 2003 Pat Ennis launched Inc Marketing Services LLC. This decision exemplifies Pat's approach to customer service which is "Say Yes" and then figure out how to get it done. IMS is now a thriving business, and Pat's first client has since grown to over $15 million in sales.

Many small business owners today struggle to build an effective advertising strategy. Pat provides his expert services as a marketing coach and public speaker. He helps clients craft and execute a marketing plan to keep and capture new business. His featured talks include advice on personal and business branding, customer service, digital marketing and sales.

Pat is based in the Washington, DC area. Before IMS, Pat held executive management positions with Fortune 500 companies and worked on campaigns at companies such as Sara Lee®, United HealthCare® and UPS®. He is also a member of the American Marketing Association.

Pat is offering readers of this book a 25 percent discount on his workshops or coaching services. Use code BSWE on the website or contact him at pat@incmarketingservices.com for more details.

Annihilate Your Phone Call Phobia

Accomplish your business goals with ease

By Linda Sturdivant

I had my dream job as a labor and delivery nurse when I learned that my third grade son was failing school. I was working the evening shift and was gone at homework time and most weekends, too. I decided to quit my job and make sure my son was successful in school. When my husband asked me, "How will we pay for the kids to go to college?" I announced that I would earn money from my direct sales business, which was a pretty idealistic announcement. Up to that point, my direct sales income had been a trickle. I heard the word *no* more often than I care to remember. For the sake of my son, I was determined to succeed and had to overcome one big challenge: Phone Call Phobia. I hated to pick up the phone.

What is Phone Call Phobia? Ask yourself if this scenario sounds familiar.

- You hear the clock ticking.
- The minute hand is steadily moving closer to the 12.
- Your stomach tightens.
- Vague waves of nausea wash over you.
- Suddenly the voice in your head says, *"That toilet really needs to be cleaned."*

71

I bet you know what time it is. Yes, it is time to make phone calls. If those descriptions sound all too familiar to you, then you might just be afflicted with Phone Call Phobia, too!

Here is the good news—there is a cure!

Intentions

In this chapter, you will discover a proven strategy that will enable you to:

- Make phone calls with ease by creating rapport with the person with whom you speak.
- Provide value to your customer right over the phone.
- Discover a proven phone call strategy to accomplish your business goals.

The Secret

The key to making phone calls with ease is to change the focus from *you* to your *customer*. Shine a spotlight on her and her needs by *asking questions*. Questions are the answer.

When you are the one asking the questions, you are in control of the conversation. The secret is to ask effective questions that uncover needs for your products or services and inspire the desire to take action.

Step One: The Opening
Your goal in Step One is to put your client at ease and differentiate yourself from an anonymous telemarketer. Get two to three positive responses and permission to talk. Here is an example:

Hi Mary, it is Linda Sturdivant calling. Now pause. The expected response can be one of these three things: *Yes? Hi Linda,* or *Who?*

Next, state a fact. For example, say: *As you recall you met me at Suzy Smith's XYZ show last week. I am your XYZ consultant.* Now pause. The expected response is *Oh, yes, I remember.*

Finally, ask permission to take her time. For example, say: *Do you have a quick minute?* Pause. The expected response is *yes* or *no.* If she says *no,* ask when is a more convenient time to call back and make sure you call her back at that time. If she says *yes,* then move forward to Step Two.

Step Two: The Reason
Give her a reason for your call and obtain permission to ask questions. For example, if this is a client you have not spoken to in some time, say: *It has been some time since we have spoken and I was thinking about you. I was wondering if I could ask you a couple of quick questions?*

If you saw her recently, include that fact. Say: *I wanted to thank you for attending Suzi's show last week.* Pause and allow her to respond. Next say something like: *I find it difficult to get to know people in a party setting and was wondering if I could ask you a couple of quick questions? Now pause for her response.*

Since she said she had time to talk, most of the time she will answer *yes* she is open to answering a couple of quick questions.

Step Three: Establish Rapport
> *"People don't care how much you know*
> *until they know how much you care."*
—John C. Maxwell, American author and leadership expert

Your client really does not care about your products or specials unless she feels she has a need for them. In Step Three, you will uncover a need and demonstrate that you care about her. This is a powerful combination to inspire clients to take action.

Question One: Initiate the conversation by asking a super simple question that assumes she needs your type of product or service. For example: *Do you wear jewelry every day or just on special occasions? Are you more of a scrap-booker or paper crafter? Do you cook dinner every night or just on the weekends?*

Question Two: Encourage her to expand her answer by asking a follow-up question, such as: *What is the next special occasion you have coming up? Are you getting as much scrapbooking done as you would like? What is the biggest challenge you have to getting a nutritious and delicious meal on the table every night?*

Paraphrase her answer back to her to make sure you are completely clear on what she said and to give her the opportunity to clarify. For example, if she says, *The next special occasion is my nephew's wedding in July,* you can respond with, *Your nephew's wedding?*

She will reply with more information: *Yes, my nephew is getting married and I guess I need to go buy a new dress to wear. I really hate to do that because I have a new dress in my closet that I have only worn once. I can't wear the exact same dress I wore last time I saw them.*

Question Three: Emotion is the mother of action. Now your goal is to have her imagine having what she wants. For example: *How would it feel to walk into your nephew's wedding wearing your beautiful dress, updated with a perfectly coordinated new jewelry ensemble?*

Listen very carefully to her answer. If she answers with an enthusiastic positive response, you have identified a need and can move to Step Four.

If she is hesitant about her answer or says *I guess that would feel good,* it indicates you have not identified a real need. Try asking, *If we could make it perfect for you, what would that look like?* Or, *If you could wave a magic wand and make it perfect, what would that look like?*

Pause and patiently wait for her reply. She will identify her need if you give her time to think.

Step Four: Make the Connection and Extend an Offer
Now that you have established rapport and identified a need, ask permission to make your offer. Say: *You know, I have some ideas about that and I would love to take just a moment so tell you about them. May I share?*

Asking permission is critically important. It helps her to transition from talking to listening. And, because you have established rapport, when you use the word *share* it will feel natural for her to say *yes.*

Tell her what you have to offer in your business and connect it to the need she has stated. Always start with the your most valuable offering. For example: *One of the services I offer is to help people coordinate their clothing with our jewelry. You could invite your friends over for a fun girl's night out and encourage each of them to bring an outfit they will be wearing to a special occasion in the upcoming months. We will have lots of fun trying on the different jewelry ensembles which will compliment their outfits. Does that sound like something you might be interested in?*

If she says *yes,* then move forward to scheduling a show.

If she says *no,* then offer a one-on-one shopping experience. For example: *Another option is for you and I to get together and I will show you some beautiful options to coordinate with your dress that you plan to wear to your nephew's wedding. We could meet at your house or my house. What would work best for you?*

If she says *yes,* then move forward to scheduling the meeting.

Continue to share whatever you have to offer in your business. This includes classes or workshops, joining your newsletter email list and so forth.

Step Five: Follow up
If you have identified a need and heard enthusiasm in her voice when you were asking questions, the chance of making an appointment is very high. However, if the answer was *no* or *not now* to everything you offered, or if she only agreed to be on the email list, schedule a follow-up phone call. Say: *I would love to follow up with you in the future. What will work best for you, a week, a month or a year?*

Make sure to schedule the follow-up call on your calendar and follow up with her at that time. Following up when you say you will creates rapport and will demonstrate you are reliable and trustworthy.

Some clients will want to do business with you right away and others will need multiple contacts with you before they are ready to take action. Follow up with your clients several times if necessary.

Prepare to Succeed

This phone call strategy is a powerful business tool which enabled me to take my business from a trickle to a swiftly moving steam of income, awards, promotions and incentive trips. It only works if you do it. Therefore, I offer the following five tips to help you make phone calls a regular part of how you build your business with ease.

1. Create a phone calling habit. Create regular time in your schedule to make phone calls. Make them at the same time each day to create a habit. After approximately three weeks of making phone calls at the same time, you will feel funny if you do not make calls.

2. Practice. Just like when you learned to drive a car or tie your shoes, this strategy can be uncomfortable at first. Practice with a friend. Practice alone in your office, saying the words out loud with the phone at your ear. Practice key phrases out loud as you drive your car or fold the laundry. It will get easier.

3. Be prepared. You do not start a recipe before making sure you have all the ingredients, right? Prepare well ahead of time by collecting the names, phone numbers and reasons for calling and have everything ready when your phone call time rolls around.

4. Create a success ritual. Have a regular routine you go through before making phone calls and repeat it each time, for example: Prepare your favorite beverage to enjoy while making phone calls.

As you walk toward your office, repeat an affirmation to yourself such as, *I am committed to customer service,* or, *I care about my clients enough to make client-focused phone calls.* This puts you in a positive frame of mind and interrupts the negative self-talk that creates Phone Call Phobia.

Open up your customer notebook or electronic customer database to make notes about your conversations while you are on the phone. Note: your customer notebook is a three-ring binder filled with lined paper. When you talk to a customer, write the date, name and phone number at the top of the page. Make notes about the phone conversation. When you are finished with the call, file the sheet under the appropriate A-Z tab in your notebook or save it electronically.

Sit down and begin making your calls.

5. Track your results. Tracking your phone calls is a powerful way to give yourself feedback about your results and to keep you focused on making enough calls. On a paper calendar—get one free at www.vertex42.com —make marks to indicate each phone call and the results. I recommend making dots on your calendar as shown:

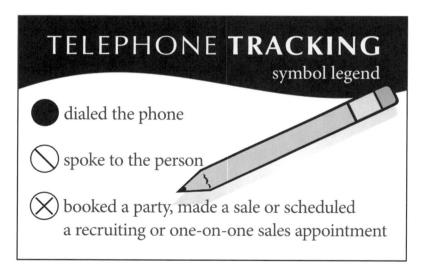

Conclusion

I encourage you to begin making client-focused phone calls on a daily basis; your business will thrive with ease. As you focus on your client, identifying her needs and connecting her with your products and services, you will find your calendar filled within a few short weeks. Your clients will become raving fans because they know you care deeply about them. Do not be surprised when clients say *thank you for calling* at the end of your phone calls. Imagine how much easier it will be to pick up the phone when you know your clients enjoy hearing from you!

Special Offer

Make your phone calls with ease with the following two free gifts:

1. A worksheet to help you craft your questions.

2. A customizable set of flash cards to use while making your calls.

Visit this special link on my website to get yours today: www.nophonefear.com/bswe

Get daily phone call tips by liking my Facebook page, just enter *No Phone Fear* in the search box.

Linda Sturdivant
Annihilate Your Phone Calling Phobia

408-265-4147
linda@nophonefear.com
www.nophonefear.com

Linda is a sought after speaker and a certified master coach who is passionate about empowering sales professionals to unleash their potential and achieve their goals. Her speeches inspire, motivate and transform audiences from being afraid to pick up the phone to taking inspired action and achieving remarkable results.

As a coach, Linda works with her clients to create a vivid vision of success. Linda offers a full array of coaching programs, including group and individual programs that incorporate assessment, strategy and accountability. Clients identify their true passion, formulate personal strategies and are held accountable to taking action, resulting in a satisfying and powerfully successful experience. With over 18 years in professional sales, Linda brings vast knowledge, a passion for learning and a dynamic personality to her speaking and coaching. Linda built a successful sales career, including earning seven incentive trips, sales and recruiting awards and building a team with $250,000 annual sales.

To schedule Linda as the speaker for your next event or to learn more about her coaching programs, please call 408-265-4147, email linda@nophonefear.com or visit www.nophonefear.com.

Discover the Secrets to Eliminating Overwhelm with Ease

By Terry Monaghan

Does anyone here ever feel overwhelmed? You are in the right place. When did our 24/7 life morph into 36/9? And why do we still have no time?

In today's fast-paced world of business and technology, everything that was supposed to be making life easier is conspiring to swallow us whole. Between smart phones, email, instant messaging, social networking, running a business, running a family and running errands—it is sometimes hard to remember to have a life.

Everyone feels overwhelmed and stressed out from time to time, and our current way of working does not help. Have you ever noticed that when you feel stressed, it is just a short hop to feeling overwhelmed? Science explains the phenomenon: when you are overwhelmed, you actually lose both your ability to focus and your ability to block out all other stimuli. That means everything is happening at once, and you are aware of it—total overload. You cannot focus on even one thing to pull yourself out. Have you ever noticed that? No wonder we feel like we are running in circles as fast as we can, getting absolutely nowhere!

In this chapter, I will bring to light some of the realities of our current situation. You will discover the biggest impediments to our productivity. I am going to share some statistics that show you why you are not crazy to feel overwhelmed and stressed out.

It is not all bad news, though. I will touch on some innovative solutions that will make a real, measurable difference—today! Finally, I will leave everyone with a simple process guaranteed to free up about two hours a day. That would add up to four months over the course of the next year. What would you do with an additional four months of productive time?

> *"Until you value yourself, you won't value your time.*
> *Until you value your time, you will not do anything with it."*
> **—M. Scott Peck, American psychiatrist**
> **and best-selling author**

Why Listen to Me?

Way back when I started my first business, I had to learn, painfully, how to deal with an overwhelming schedule. I was working very long hours. In fact, it was not unusual to work all night to get a project done for a client. At the same time, I was attending graduate school. This meant hours each week attending class, and even more hours studying and writing research papers. During the last six months of my graduate program, I was also participating in an intensive leadership development program, with even more hours of work that needed to be crammed in somehow.

At that point, it looked like the only way I was going to get everything done was to either:

1. Find some serious drugs (which was not really an option)

2. Give up sleeping (also not a viable option)

3. Give up either work, school, the leadership course or my social life (did not want to do that) or

4. Figure out a better way!

I knew that the only way I was going to survive was if I took complete control of my schedule. Through a little trial and error, I discovered what was contributing to the overwhelm. That helped me approach my schedule in a way that brought me a lot of sanity, while at the same time allowed me to pursue all the different interests I had.

That is what I share with you in this chapter. I have learned how to master how I use time, while ensuring time for a life and achieving great business results. It is the most valuable skill I ever learned. And it is one skill I pass on to every single one of my clients.

To be Successful, Time is a Serious Issue

Talent and hard work do not always equal success. Many talented business people flounder, while only a handful truly succeed. What secret do the successful people know that allows them to profit from their talents? The answer is simple: successful people have become masters of time. They have mastered their schedules.

Let me give you a personal example of my formula in action.

In a recent three-month period, I attended two week-long business conferences, designed and hosted a business intensive, planned and launched a public workshop, conducted interviews with sixteen experts for a Master Class series, wrote three-quarters of a book and began working with four new private clients.

It is important to note that I did not work evenings nor weekends during this time. I take my down time very seriously. I love and need that time for reading, relaxing, puttering, spending time with friends and family, playing with my cats or just doing nothing.

Here is an even more compelling example from a client. She is a successful real estate agent. She was already producing about $20 million in transactions a year before we began working together. At the time, she was working seven days a week, including evenings. She could see that she was on the verge of sacrificing precious time with her family, with no end in sight.

We examined every single activity in her daily plan and created a schedule and a structure that allowed her to meet her professional goals—and still have time to focus on what was most important to her. The end result? Five years of spectacular growth in her real estate practice, more time with friends and family, time for giving back in her community and regularly scheduled down time, including vacations where she completely unplugs.

Why Are We So Overwhelmed?

I have worked with hundreds of professionals, executives and entrepreneurs since 1998. These are some of the most common time killers many of us have to deal with:

- **You do not know why you are doing what you are doing—or why it is important to do it.** You have not created a strategy for what you are doing. You do not know how it fits into the bigger picture of what you want to accomplish. This makes it look like one more to-do in an already overflowing list of things to do. One example here is social media. You have heard you should be on Facebook®, LinkedIn® and Twitter®, that you should be blogging and reading blogs—and you should be doing it often! Really? Without a strategy, without knowing exactly what you want to produce from these activities, you are left wondering, *When exactly am I supposed to be doing all of that? 3:00 a.m.? I think I have some time then.*

- **You look for things.** Do you have any idea how much time you spend each day just looking for something you need? It could be a file, a phone number, a document, it does not matter what it is. Workplace studies indicate we spend, on average, 45 minutes every day looking for a misplaced item. That is 9 percent of the average 8-hour workday, which adds up to about six weeks every year—six weeks spent looking for things!

- **You try to get through your email inbox.** How many of you have more than 100 messages in your inbox? More than 1,000? More than 5,000? Does it just make you tired to even think about it? Based on a series of surveys done in Fortune 500 companies, experts have estimated that the average businessperson spends up to three hours per day sorting email. This does not include doing any of the work the email generates. If you do the math—three hours a day, 52 weeks a year—it adds up to 19.5 weeks every year spent sorting email. According to 2012 figures, this same business person now receives the equivalent of a 250-page book every single day.

- **You allow interruptions.** Statistics indicate that on average, we are interrupted at least once every six to eight minutes, and it can take as long as fifteen minutes to resume the task at hand (assuming we remember what it was). Let us look at that—you get interrupted every six minutes and it takes fifteen minutes to bring your focus back. However, before you can bring your focus back to the task at hand, you are interrupted again. That means the day's first interruption can derail your entire day! Has this happened to you?

- **You attend unnecessary meetings.** How many meetings have you attended where you realized that the entire thing could have been handled with one or two emails or a short conference call? Perhaps you were in a meeting for one or two hours and absolutely nothing got done. Depending on where you are in the hierarchy of your organization, it is entirely possible that thirty to ninety percent of your time could be spent in meetings. Another study of Fortune 500 executives revealed that many of them felt lucky if they had twenty-eight to forty-five minutes of productive, focused time each day.

- **You struggle with inefficient processes.** You try to remember how you do things, yet have not taken the time to write it down. Perhaps you are following some complicated 35-step procedure that could be done in five steps because *that is the way we have always done it.*
- **You try to do it all—and do it all yourself.** How is that working for you?

Where does that leave us? So far, we have accounted for over 100 percent of your time, and we have not gotten any work done.

We are playing an unwinnable game, in an unworkable environment and we really do not have any time left! Given these circumstances, I believe we are already amazingly productive. The tragedy, of course, is it takes us eight hours to accomplish those forty-five minutes of true productivity each day. No wonder we feel overwhelmed and under constant stress!

How to Manage Your Time—and Create Business Success with Ease
I am going to give you some simple solutions to address each of these areas. While they are simple, they are not necessarily easy to implement—just know that any one of them will produce a measurable result immediately!

Plan Your Strategy

What, exactly, do you intend to accomplish by doing x, y or z? For example, when I decided to jump into social media, my strategy was to use it to increase my visibility in the business community. I created a way to be on people's radar once a day. I also found a site that let me pre-schedule status updates and share the same updates to several platforms at once. Initially, I budgeted about one hour a week. What was the result? My list of contacts increased. I began hearing from people I met networking, "Oh, I've heard of you!" I would say that was a successful, timesaving strategy!

Get Organized

Reduce the time you spend looking for what you need by getting organized. Close your eyes and picture your primary workspace. Got it? Good. Now ask yourself if it is set up in such a way that it invites you in and allows you to get real work done, or if it is it set up in such a way that it compels you to run screaming from the building. The easiest way to do this is to work with a professional organizer. Let's face it—if you knew what to do to get organized, you would have already done it. I want to clear up one thing here—having a neat office does not necessarily mean you have an organized office. Some of the most organized people I know have untidy offices, however everything has a logic to it and they can find what they need exactly when they need it.

Establish a Process for Dealing with Your Email

In Brendon Bruchard's book *The Millionaire Messenger,* published by Morgan James in March 2011, the author says that your email inbox is a perfectly organized collection of everyone else's agenda. Let's bring the focus back to your agenda, shall we?

This is the simple process I promised to tell you about at the beginning of the chapter. Set a specific time each day when you check your email.

Turn off the function that pushes email to your computer or smart phone. When it is time to check, pull all the messages into the inbox.

Go through and sort everything in one pass. Do not try to sort some and work on some—for now just sort. Here are some criteria:

- Read and delete
- Read and respond
- Read and schedule for future action
- Divert—create a rule to automatically sort mail into separate folders that you can access as you have time

Shifting from checking your email every three to seven minutes throughout the day to checking two to three times a day will free up an average of two hours every day, immediately.

Finally, stop treating email as if it were a form of instant message.

Managing Interruptions

Dan Kennedy, marketing expert and author of *No BS Time Management for Entrepreneurs,* published in 2004 by Entrepreneur Press, says, "If they can't find you, they can't interrupt you." Consider tackling your most important task of the day before you check your email and your voicemail. Do not be afraid to close your door—put a sign on it if you need to—so you can focus on your work. The world will not end if you let your phone calls go to voicemail. You can manage people's expectations by recording a clear message that lets them know when you will return calls, or setting up an email auto-response that tells people how often you check your inbox. This way you will not get six messages asking why you have not responded to the first.

If you only have 45 minutes of productive time in the day, why not get those 45 minutes in and your most important actions done first thing—before anyone has a chance to interrupt?

Meetings

What is the intended outcome of the meeting? Can it be accomplished with a phone call? If yes, then do that and save everyone time. If you must have a meeting, be certain there is a clearly stated outcome, an agenda and a firm start and end time. Create clear action items before you end the meeting. A meeting that does not produce action items was probably unnecessary.

Ineffective Processes

Do not be afraid to ask *why* when you find yourself wondering if the way something is being done makes sense. Why are we doing it this way? Is there a better, simpler way to get the same result? Are we using our technology to the fullest? Often, we are too involved in what we are doing to step back to see if there might be a better way. If you find yourself operating with a sense of frustration and anxiety, you may want to take a step back. Look at what is being done and how it is being done—see if you can tell where it has fallen apart. An outside pair of eyes is great here, too.

Delegate!

Take the time to identify the best, most leveraged use of your time. What do you do that really puts money in your pocket, that gives you great joy and satisfaction? What do you do that is your own unique brilliance? Focus on that and delegate the rest. Really.

Your Next Step

In summary, the key to managing overwhelm is by controlling the areas where you actually have control. You can set boundaries. You can schedule your time. You can plan your work. You can establish processes and protocols for how things get done. You can recognize that we have created an environment where it is just not possible for one person to get it all done. Choose what you will focus on—what is most important to you—and move forward.

Terry Monaghan
Time Triage™
Improve Performance | Produce Results |
Increase Revenue

703-829-5097
terry@timetriage.com
www.timetriage.com

Before launching her business, Terry Monaghan, founder and CEO of Time Triage™, invested years being trained and developed in distinctions of planning, time management, leadership and coaching others to produce results while producing extraordinary results herself. She is well versed in the theories behind what impacts performance and productivity, yet she is far more interested in creating custom solutions for her clients that create a measurable difference today.

With more than thirty years of business and entrepreneurial experience, Terry's unique technology has dramatically increased the productivity of Fortune 100 executives, entrepreneurs and professionals. Whether you are a corporate executive or a solo-preneur, the outcome of Terry's methodology will give you an expanded level of freedom and productivity with results you can measure. Terry's clients find themselves working on what is most fulfilling and what really matters in moving things forward rather than what they previously thought they "had to do." Under her guidance, the things you hoped to get to someday become the things you work on today.

To determine your next steps toward the success you deserve, visit www.timetriage.com to schedule a private Productivity Breakthrough Session.

Creating Successful Systems and Implementing with Ease

By Bibi Goldstein

Why do you need systems? Because no one can see what is going on inside your head. Creating a systematic approach to every part of your business, regardless of size, allows you to grow with greater ease. As an entrepreneur or small business owner, you probably do not like dealing with these not so sexy, yet fundamentally necessary, components of your business.

If you think about creating a system around everything that makes your business run, down to the simplest of things like how you answer the phone, your ability for growth with minimal pain and expenses increases exponentially.

Most businesses spend many intangible dollars on delegation. Whether delegating to an employee, consultant or vendor, we train and educate hoping that they work out. If they do not, then we find someone else to train, hoping that they work out. This cycle just continues the more we grow.

Do you know how much time and money that really is when someone does not work out in your business? More importantly, given all the expenses you have, can you afford not to know what this critical part of your business is costing you? Just because you are not writing yourself a check for that training does not mean there is not a cost to it.

Have you done the time: value: money equation to see what your time is worth, and how much of the time you spend training—or worse—re-doing a trainee's work? How much are you spending in dollars weekly, monthly or annually in delegating work? If you do not know the answer to this question, find out fast.

It is time for you to start focusing on systemizing and delegating the aspects of your business that are holding you back.

> *"If you can't describe what you are doing as a process,*
> *you don't know what you're doing."*
> **—W. Edwards Deming, American statistician**

Implementing Systems for Your Business
Can Be Easy, Especially if You Start from Day One

Here is a simple-to-follow outline for documenting a process. For the purpose of providing actual content, we will use the example of answering the phone. When creating this document, you can use templates available online. You can also use a Word document with bullet points and the six key elements outlined below. Using print screen images in the document whenever possible is always helpful for the trainee.

1. What. Indicate the name of the process. Whenever possible, if you have a company policy that can be identified that goes hand-in-hand with this process, please do so here.

Example: *To answer all calls during business hours in a courteous and helpful way as our customer service policy outlines.*

2. Why. Give a description of the purpose of this process.

Example: *Our customer service policy is to serve our customers in the most efficient, empathetic and exceptional way to leave them feeling we did all possible to handle their issue even if it was not the outcome they envisioned.*

3. Who. Identify the staff position within your company that handles this process.

Example: *Primarily handled by the receptionist, with all other staff members providing back up, and finally to voicemail if, and only if, staff is not available.*

4. When. How often does this process occur and at what time of day?

Example: *Monday through Friday, 8:30 a.m. to 5:00 p.m. Pacific time except pre-determined holidays.*

5. Where. This is where you will need to put any specific location areas or any URLs with logins or passwords that are needed.

Example: *Calls are routed via www.grasshopper.com login: 3105551111 password or pin: 2012*

6. How. Here is where step-by-step instructions will need to be clearly written and screen shots can be provided. Each step should be on its own line, with a space between each step.

Example:
Step 1—The call will come in.
Step 2—Answer the call by pressing 1.
Step 3—Say, "Thank you for calling ABC Widget, this is Cathy. How may I assist you?"
Step 4—Handle the request of the caller or transfer to the appropriate department/person by pressing ## then following the prompts.

Step 5—Whenever taking a message, always email that message with the subject line of "Phone Message: Cindy Williams called @10:30 a.m." Include the actual message information in the body of the email.

Using Technology to Automate

Delegating to technology rather than an individual is an option every business should implement. There are many things you do in your business that can be automated, even if it is only a portion of the overall process.

Establishing systems in some very basic areas can help minimize your time spent on processes that are necessary to keep your business moving forward. Here are some options to consider:

- **Accounting.** Whether you want to go old school and use a spreadsheet to manage your accounting needs or use systems that manage it for you, there are several options. Microsoft® Excel, Smartsheet®, Quicken™, Quickbooks™, Freshbooks®. For most business owners, Quickbooks® (online or desktop) or Freshbooks would be ideal.
- **Scheduling/calendar management.** Having an online calendar that can be shared is crucial when working with multiple people. In addition to allowing for more efficiencies in determining best times to meet, it can also provide a way for your staff and even your family to know your availability if they need to schedule time with you. There are also scheduling systems that allow your customers to book appointment times directly with you once you have predetermined your availability. Some of the more popular programs are, Google™ Calendar, Schedulicity® and TimeTrade®.
- **Project management.** If you have multiple projects and multiple people handling specific tasks within a project, it is imperative that you have a means to manage these projects. Do your homework and

determine what you really need, as the features vary a great deal. One Place®, Basecamp® and Central Desktop® are great options, however not all of them provide time tracking.

- **Electronic contract management.** Contracts and proposals are a big part of some businesses, and the process of getting them out to prospects, then delivering signed and fully executed copies back to each party, could become cumbersome. DocuSign® and EchoSign® are just a couple of examples of systems that can streamline and expedite this process. Please be sure to check with your local laws to determine the validity of an electronic signature. In the state of California, for example, electronic signatures are recognized as a legal and binding signature.

- **Email marketing.** If you do any type of email marketing to your customers—from a monthly newsletter to more complicated campaigns based on your customer or prospect behaviors—do not use your regular email system (Gmail®, Yahoo®, Microsoft® Outlook or others). There are easy to use systems out there like MailChimp® and Constant Contact®. Some are a little more intricate, like AWeber® and 1ShoppingCart®—and then there is the sophisticated Infusionsoft®. Whichever program you decide to use, make sure you understand CAN-SPAM laws and are communicating in a consistent and strategic manner.

- **Customer relationship management (CRM).** Every business should have a way to manage how and when they interact with customers. If there is an event that occurs between you and a customer—whether it is a phone call, email or an in-person meeting—that should be documented in a CRM system. This is especially important if there are multiple people on your team interacting with the same customer. The ability to view the background and history allows you to better serve your customer by knowing what has actually happened and what needs special attention because a similar situation might have happened in the past. There are multiple CRMs available like Salesforce® or

Infusionsoft. Find the one that is right for your business in the long term, try not to go with something that will "work for now."

Establishing Personal Processes and Systems

As important as it is to have systems and processes in your business, it is equally important to have a systematic approach to your own personal processes.

As a business owner, your time and responsibilities often get put aside for the sake of others. When you get behind with your own work, there is a vicious cycle it creates for your entire business. Your ability to get things done will directly reflect whether you are the bottleneck in your own organization.

There are some proven techniques that can help keep you focused, on task and on time.

- **Day blocking.** Set your days up for specific functions that give you the opportunity to work on your business rather than in it. Here is an example of how day blocking could be set up:

  Monday: Customer project work, financial related activities, huddles (explanation of this later in this section), no appointments

  Tuesday: All appointments (customers, vendors) by phone or in person, customer project work

  Wednesday: All appointments (customers, vendors by phone only, marketing and branding activities (website content updates and more), business education (reading e-zines, newsletters, blogs, books, trainings, webinars)

  Thursday: Writing (blogs, articles), all appointments (customers, vendors) by phone or in person (afternoon only)

  Friday: Customer project work, huddles, no appointments

Keep in mind that these are guidelines, especially for your team, therefore they and you can make certain that those areas a CEO needs to focus on have a time of priority.

- **Time blocking.** Use your calendar for more than just maintaining appointments: create time blocks for projects and the other areas outlined in your day blocking. Here is an example of a time blocking set up:

8:30 a.m. to 10:00 a.m., Email

10:00 a.m. to 1:00 p.m., Appointments

1:00 p.m. to 2:00 p.m., Marketing and Branding

2:00 p.m. to 3:00 p.m., Email

3:00 p.m. to 5:00 p.m., Business Education

As you can see, this is not a full day's calendar or schedule. This simply identifies priorities for the day and when they will be done.

- **15-minute blocking.** As business owners, there are many little things you simply must do in order to stay organized and focused on the big picture. This technique of chipping away at things 15 minutes at a time will allow you to see progress over time and create systems for those areas that you dread doing. Here is an example of a 15-minute blocking set up:

Monday: Desk de-clutter, sorting paper piles

Tuesday: Sorting paper piles, networking or event follow-up

Wednesday: Email clean up, networking or event follow-up, desk de-clutter

Thursday: Sorting paper piles, computer document or desktop clean-up

Friday: Email clean-up, desk de-clutter

A few hints when doing your 15 minutes in any of these areas: set a timer and only work for 15 minutes. Even if you are on a roll and want to keep going, stop. If you have the ability, each morning put the 15 minutes into your calendar for the specific time you will do each item. Turn everything else off except the timer or whatever you need to work on. If you can give yourself and the task at hand your full attention for 15 minutes, it will make a huge impact. One last note: if you have piles that need to be sorted before you can take future action, do not work on an entire pile to see what you can accomplish in those 15 minutes. Instead, tackle no more than two inches worth of paper at one time. Use different colored Post it® Notes to identify for your team or yourself what you have sorted and the next step for those papers.

- **Huddles.** These are opportunities for you to stay in touch with your team (on-site assistant, virtual assistant, employees) on a regular basis so that everyone has an opportunity to discuss the good, the bad and the ugly. When you first start these, they might last thirty minutes, however the goal is to get these down to fifteen minutes. Hold huddles at the beginning and end of each week. Use this formula during those huddles:

Good: three minutes. Discuss one or maybe two specific positive areas related to the work the person you are huddling with is involved.

Bad: five minutes. Discuss one or maybe two specific issues that might have occurred where there is a need to correct or revise a process.

Ugly: five minutes. Discuss one specific issue that requires addressing with a customer or team member that was a complete deviation from your policies or procedures.

Good: three minutes. Wrap up on a positive note, maybe with a concrete action plan to address the "ugly" issue, or maybe provide some positive feedback received from a customer.

This is often referred to as the sandwich method and you can always think of the bread as the "good" part. If you choose to do thirty-minute huddles, simply double the time for each area. One last note is to make sure the person you are huddling with is taking notes and identifying any action items. Make it a regular practice to require that within fifteen minutes of the end of the huddle, those notes are sent to you.

No matter what your processes, systems, technology or overall management style is, the most important ingredient is consistency. Maintaining consistency will allow you greater freedom from reacting and give you the opportunity to be proactive with your team and your customers.

Just Do Something, Anything, One Thing

Find one area that you can implement at a time, maybe one per month. Try not to focus on what did not happen exactly as it is outlined here. Instead, focus on what you were able to get accomplished. After all, the goal is that by having a systematic approach to all areas of your business, you can continue to grow without the pain.

Bibi Goldstein

Buying Time, LLC

Supporting business owners through strategic planning and virtual assistance

310-376-1835
bibi@buyingtimellc.com
www.buyingtimellc.com

During a 22-year career in transportation and logistics, Bibi Goldstein never thought of herself as an entrepreneur...until she launched Buying Time, LLC in 2007. Today she serves more than 200 clients globally, with services ranging from administrative needs, email marketing, time management, procedures implementation and maintenance and strategic planning.

Bibi speaks on Time Management to Systems and Delegation. She conducts workshops and virtual courses on email management and de-cluttering. Bibi is an active member of her Southern California business community. She is past-president of the South Bay Business Women's Association and committee member and past chair for the Manhattan Beach Women in Business. She is past-president of the Kiwanis Club of Manhattan Beach and a member of the 2011 class of Leadership Redondo.

Bibi is a co-author of another Thrive publication, *Get Organized Today*. She is also a contributing expert to *Today's Innovative Woman* magazine. Bibi lives in Redondo Beach with her husband, Mark. Her daughter, Julie, studies business and marketing at San Francisco State.

Visit www.buyingtimellc.com to get your free copy of the *Productivity Blueprint* system. This will help you identify your productivity time zone so you manage your time and projects more efficiently.

Your Image Is Talking About You

Be Authentic—Be Intentional—Be Successful

By Kasey Roberts Smith

"To thine own self be true."
—William Shakespeare, English poet and playwright

I magine . . . you are about to walk into a business meeting. The conference room is full of people who can help make your next project a success. You want to make a great first impression so they will see you as credible, reliable and trustworthy. However, before you say a word, your *Appearance, Behavior* and non-verbal *Communication* are transmitting messages about you whether you are aware of them or not. Sometimes those messages interfere with your success.

As human beings, we are walking billboards, transmitting information about ourselves that is subconsciously picked up by others. We are hard-wired to make snap judgments about our environment. This has to do with our fight, flight or freeze responses. It is a subconscious mechanism that is supposed to keep us safe, out of harm's way. Even when we are safe—no real or metaphorical lions, tigers or bears chasing us—this built-into-our-genes assessment tool kicks in, and we judge everything around us.

This is why first impressions are made in ten seconds or less. It does not seem fair, does it? It is just the way we are wired. We are all connected. We are all intuitive. We sense when someone is being genuine, if their message is congruent and vice versa. Being aware of these messages and the impact they have on our reputation is paramount in projecting the image we want to share with the world.

I invite you to take a closer look at the messages you are sending out into the world through your *Appearance, Behavior* and *Communication*—your image. Small shifts in any of these can make a big difference in your confidence level and, therefore, give you more business success with ease.

My Story

My interest in this subject began when I was a very young girl, although I did not know it was called "image" at the time. I grew up in a rodeo family and was quite aware that western clothing was different from city clothing. I was a girly girl rather than a tomboy and wanted to wear more feminine garments.

I began sewing very early on and loved to experiment with patterns and fabric to create what I wanted to wear. I enrolled in fashion merchandising classes and later received my degree in both fashion design and pattern drafting.

Much of the focus in design school was on trends, high fashion runway shows and the size four dress form. I knew that was not my market. When I added image training to my education, I realized it was the individual who mattered, not mass production. Nor was it about color and fashion trends; it was about what looks best on each individual person.

Image consulting, for me, is first and foremost about individuality and authenticity. It is about working with you directly to discover your core essence, define your personal color, style and fit aesthetic and then help you build a wardrobe that matches your lifestyle and tells your story.

The ABCs of Image

Your image is more than just your physical *Appearance*. It also encompasses your *Behavior*—how you act and deal with people, as well as your *Communication* skills and body language—how you talk to people. All three are integrated into your image because all three are expressed as you interact with people. You cannot isolate one from the other or say one is more important than the other because all three represent who you are from the inside out.

General topics under the ABCs of Image:
- *Appearance*—color, style, fit, wardrobe, grooming, closets, shopping
- *Behavior*—etiquette (dining and business), social skills, civility, protocol
- *Communication*—presentation skills, body language, personal branding

Making a great impression is about making a connection, being likable and creating rapport. Trust, very needed in business today, comes after you build rapport. Congruency in your verbal and non-verbal messages is vitally important. The ABCs of Image is an excellent place to check yourself for consistency.

Essence + Intention + Presence = Magic

Essence is another word to describe your core nature. It is your vibrational frequency, your innate personality, the drumbeat or rhythm of your soul. When you surround yourself in color, clothing and accessories that are a match to your essence, your true beauty shines through.

Intention is your course of action to accomplish your goals. You have heard the expression, "act as if." This principle works for "dress as if" also. When you dress like the person you see yourself becoming—or for the position you are seeking—you create that in your life. You are "visually" affirming your intended outcome. The secret is that your intention must align and be harmonious with your essence for it to be authentic.

Presence is another word to describe your image, the distinctive manner of your outward expression. It is the visual articulation of who you are. Presence is the source of the messages you send out to the world—where first impressions originate.

The more you define your core essence and express yourself authentically, the more connected you are to yourself and others. You are more relatable, congruent and memorable. You are heard more effectively and seen as credible, reliable and trustworthy.

This blending of your essence, intention and presence is also called your personal brand. When all three are aligned—magic happens!

Personal Branding

Personal branding is a hot topic in the marketplace today. A brand is more than a logo. It is the reputation of the person behind the brand that is important.

I remember my first exposure to branding. It was my grandfather's livestock brand that I saw every day while I was growing up. He was a rodeo stock contractor. His brand was designed from his initials, ECR, for EC Roberts. His brand stood for integrity, honesty and dependability. His word was his bond; his handshake was his contract. His reputation preceded him in all his business dealings.

The next generation of brands became the logos behind the labels—Coca-Cola®, Apple®, Ralph Lauren® and others. These brands also stand on reputation. Their messages should be congruent with what they deliver.

It is the same with personal branding. Whatever your brand attributes are, they must be congruent with who you are. I recommend choosing three to seven words that represent your core values and intentions. Then, refer to them when making decisions about your business and your image.

Your Radiance Signature™ Defined

Radiance literally means sending out rays of light. *Signature* refers to your mark, your style, your identity, your character. Your radiance (light) emits a vibrational frequency that is unique to you. Your Radiance Signature™ is comprised of your innate, inherent, and intrinsic attributes—the descriptive qualities of your essence and radiant light (color).

Resonance (sound frequency) is another way to describe these qualities because there is a correlation between sound and color (light). Musical notes each have a color with which they resonate. Geometric shapes and metals resonate with both sound and light and are important to you in regard to your clothing and jewelry choices.

These qualities are better understood using a familiar metaphor: the four seasons. Temperament and personality assessments have been around for thousands of years using a matrix of four. In 1942, Suzanne Caygill, pioneer of color analysis, founded her four-season color harmony system. Inspired by the four seasons of nature, this system is based on essence first—who you are on the inside—and personal coloring second. The four seasons expand to 64 different subtypes, creating a myriad of possible nuances and color palettes—a customized color system.

Read through the following list and "feel" which words resonate with you the most.

SPRING	SUMMER	AUTUMN	WINTER
CRISP	SOFT	TEXTURED	SMOOTH
ANIMATED	RELAXED	DYNAMIC	FIRM
BRIGHT	MUTED	RICH	BOLD
SPIRITED	SUBTLE	SUBSTANTIAL	STATUESQUE
SUNNY	BLENDED	EARTHY	STRIKING
PLAYFUL	GRACEFUL	INTENSE	TRANQUIL
BUOYANT	FLOWING	SWIFT	STILL
FUN	CURVED	ANGLED	CONTRAST
WHIMSICAL	POISED	SPICY	REGAL
FRESH	DELICATE	TENACIOUS	PRECISE
EFFERVESCENT	FINESSE	FLAMBOYANT	OPULENT
RADIANT	ROMANTIC	RESOURCEFUL	REFLECTIVE

You may see yourself in all four, yet one or two will resonate with you more than the others. Allow yourself to remember your essence when you were a child—before "life" covered up some of your innate and intrinsic tendencies.

You can use other names to represent these inherent qualities instead of the seasons—changing the metaphor—however, the descriptions are the same. It is the experience, the connection, the sense of wholeness that resonates within you that describes, then defines, your Radiance Signature™.

Mother Nature's Qualities

Just as Mother Nature has her perfect color palette depending on the season or the terrain, so do you. Reflected in her beauty are patterns, rhythms and cycles that are also seen in human nature and anatomy. Some of these include line, shape, color, texture, fabrication, contrast, scale, emphasis, proportion, balance, repetition and movement.

All of these play a part in your clothing choices. The secret is understanding your physicality, then repeating the design elements that are a match to you. Just as you have your Radiance Signature™, so does everything in the universe. It is like tuning in to the right radio frequency or connecting to the right URL address. When your frequency is in alignment with your clothing and embellishment—details that are a match to you—you are connected. You look radiant, alive, attractive and beautiful.

Your Color

You were born in perfect harmony, from the coloring of your skin, hair and eyes, to the energy frequencies that resonate from your soul. You are harmonious, unique and authentic.

Problems arise when you wear colors that are not in harmony with your personal coloring. Each color has its own descriptive quality called Chroma. This describes the intensity of the color as pure (brightest), washed, tinted, toned (muted or toasted) and shaded. Color analysis is about finding the right tint, tone, shade, or pure color that is right for you.

Begin wearing your personal colors—the colors in your hair, eyes and skin. Look closely—there are many colors in all three. Your predominant natural hair color is one of your foundation neutrals. If your hair is dark, it may be your formal neutral; if light, it is an informal neutral. Wearing your eye color gives you a sense of balance and centeredness. Being centered gives you credibility and favor in negotiating with ease.

The highlight colors in your eyes and rim color add more depth and dimension to the colors in your palette. The whites of your eyes, in addition to your teeth, give you your range of whites. Wearing your skin-tone color grounds you and is quite calming. It is the color that ties all your other colors together. Your "red" comes from your skin-tone. It is literally your blood flowing under your skin showing through. Depending on your coloring, it can range from the purest intense colors of red to their softest tints, tones and darkest shades. Your dramatic colors are your "wow" colors and complement every other color on your palette.

Having your color palette done is a great investment because it reveals your very best colors. These include your personal colors, neutrals, whites, reds and dramatics—including your power color—subdued colors, pastels, prints, patterns and metals. Wearing your best colors will make you look younger, thinner and healthy. Wearing colors that are wrong for you will make you look older, heavier and sickly.

Your Style

Your style is the manner in which you put your clothing and accessories together. It is your story expressed visually through the clothes you choose to wear and how you choose to wear them. It is your design aesthetic, put together your way.

Having style is about having a point of view—a cohesive look—built with basic and classic pieces that work together. It is about using accessories and other embellishments to create different looks, and adding great investment pieces to keep your look updated and current.

Having style is about being comfortable wearing your clothes and being confident in your selections. It is about knowing what is right for you and what is not right for you. It is also about having the conviction to buy only what works on your body, regardless of trends.

Having style is about having the right accessories—shoes, handbags, scarves, jewelry and glasses. Choose those pieces that make you happy, give you confidence and tell your story.

Having style is also about buying those dramatic, fantastic, one-of-a-kind pieces that really fit in with your personal style. Even if it is a trendy item, have fun with it, enjoy it. Express yourself!

Having style is not about spending a lot of money. It is about being creative—mixing items together that interest you and make *you* interesting and unique. It is about creating your Signature Look.

Your Fit

Your clothes need to fit you properly. They should hang straight from your shoulder line and skim the outline of your body with no pulling, puckering, gapping or bagging.

Alterations are a must when a garment does not fit correctly. Men typically know they have to tailor their clothes. Women tend to think clothes should fit right off the rack—and when they do not fit, they think something is wrong with them, not the clothes. It is not you. All brands have different sizing and fit specifications. Embrace your body. Discover what brands fit you and your design aesthetic. Even these clothes may need alterations.

Find a good tailor or seamstress and get familiar with what that person can do for you. Then, when you find an item you love, you will know if it can be altered or not.

A less-expensive yet good-fitting garment will enhance your image more than an expensive garment that does not fit you properly. It is the finer attention to detail that makes the difference in looking put together or thrown together.

Your Wardrobe

It is time to assess your closet—and delete, delete, delete! If you have a closet full of clothes and nothing to wear, it is time to de-stress and de-clutter! Let go of the pieces that you do not wear, do not fit you, and do not look good on you. Assess what is left and again, decide if anything else needs to go. Your closet will serve you better if it is full of pieces that connect you to your style aesthetic, your essence, and your personal coloring.

Think capsule dressing—eight to twelve pieces that mix and match, creating several different outfits, several different looks. Each capsule has a color theme: a neutral, a dramatic and a print. It is built with five core pieces: jackets, tops, skirts, dresses and pants. Accessories set the tone for each combination and can cross over to other capsules for even more options. Your capsule pieces can take you from morning to evening, season to season, and set you free from worrying about what to wear. Start by identifying items you already have that a capsule can be built upon. You probably have combinations in your closet already that you have not seen yet. Then, make a list of items you need to complete your capsule and go shopping.

Building a wardrobe is a journey. It takes time to discover, define and refine your design aesthetic, understand your physicality and colors, choose the correct silhouettes and design elements that are a match for you, and shop.

You can do it. Pace yourself and have fun!

Your Image

Your image is talking about you. It is time to find out what it is saying.

I have shared what image is and why it is important to your business success. If you would like to learn more about how to implement these ideas, I would love to work with you.

I am here to help you discover the magic of *color, style* and *fit* so that you are empowered to create a *wardrobe* you love that:

- Harmonizes with both your inner and outer beauty
- Reflects your personality, style, energy and core values
- Mixes basic and classic pieces with your favorite accessories
- Integrates fashion-forward items so your look is current
- Offers a myriad of options
- Creates an outfit for every occasion
- Represents your personal and professional presence
- Reveals your authenticity, intentions and success

The result: you are confident and ready, knowing you look great, feel comfortable and can focus on your business without wardrobe distractions.

Doing the work necessary to build your wardrobe—both professional and personal—will pay off in every area of your life. Socrates said it best: "Know thyself." When you know who you are and where you want to go, it makes it a whole lot easier to get there. With the right professional wardrobe, you will get there in style, giving you more business success with ease.

Image is all about being authentic. There is no one more powerful than a woman who knows who she is and lives her life authentically.

To get started, go to www.artistryofimage.com/bsweoffer and download your free report, *Understanding Your Physicality*.

Kasey Roberts Smith
Artistry of Image
Be The Living Work of Art That You Are™

214-837-1814
kasey@artistryofimage.com
www.artistryofimage.com

Kasey Roberts Smith, Image Consultant and Color Specialist, has a background in fashion merchandising, double degrees in fashion design and pattern drafting, and is the past owner of a costume rental and design company. When she added image consulting to the mix, she had an epiphany: Fashion is about Clothing...Image is about People!

For Kasey, the work is about helping each person connect with her true essence and then communicate that message through her *Appearance, Behavior* and *Communication*—the ABCs of Image.

Kasey is a graduate of London Image Institute, Appearance Design Institute, and Sci-Art Global. She is a member of the Association of Image Consultants International (AICI) and Colour Designers International (CDI). She is a certified mentor through Women of Visionary Influence (WOVI). Kasey is a professional speaker, trainer and workshop facilitator. She is also a member of Toastmasters International, Speaker Co-op of Dallas, National Speakers Association, and National Speakers Association North Texas.

Kasey's company is Artistry of Image. She believes we are all living works of art—masterpieces, actually—some of us just need a little tweaking!

The Power of
Professional Etiquette

By Lynda Jean, MSW, AICI

I s professional etiquette really that important to succeed in today's modern workplace?

Absolutely. Good manners are alive and well today. Who decides what good manners entail? We do. Unlike the past, manners no longer have to do with whether you are rich, had a private school education or grew up in a certain social class. Today we live in a more egalitarian society, where good manners are expected from everyone. Can you imagine people storming the gate agent at the airport, rather than waiting their turn in line? There would be chaos, resulting in angry people and inefficient business practices.

When we do not practice good manners, we often sense that we do not fit in. In the business world, people who respect their colleagues and clients are noticed, which always enhances our professional presence.

While it may seem that some people are naturals, professional etiquette is something that most people have worked hard to achieve.

In this chapter, I will cover many of the important comportment issues that convey a respectful, professional presence in the workplace. Regardless of your position in the workplace, this information applies to everyone.

When you think of professional etiquette, think of three important parts, or what I call the ABCs of good manners. These ABCs are:

- Appearance
- Behavior
- Communication

Enhance Your Appearance

Eye Contact. Making eye contact sixty to seventy percent of the time creates a sense of emotional connection.

> *"The eye obeys the action of the mind."*
> **—Ralph Waldo Emerson, American essayist,**
> **lecturer and poet**

Confident eye contact conveys two messages—I am confident and so are you. When you have good eye contact, listening attentively is easier, and when you are engaged in what the person is saying, good eye contact comes naturally. Poor eye contact communicates negative messages, such as a lack of interest in the person or in his or her information.

When you are nervous or stressed, your eye contact is affected. A helpful trick I have used when feeling nervous is to look at the area between the person's eyebrows. You will appear to be looking at their eyes, and this will give you time to gather your thoughts.

Lastly, do not forget to smile when appropriate—people always feel comfortable around those who smile.

Posture. Many of us are unaware of what our posture conveys because we do not see ourselves in interactions. Observe yourself in the mirror or ask a friend to assess your posture. People who walk with a purpose, that is, with an erect stride, are identified as secure and having something to contribute.

Sitting forward in a meeting conveys that you are interested and engaged, while crossing your arms and slouching suggest defensiveness and disinterest.

Personal Grooming. Image should not matter, but it does. Research has demonstrated over and over again that first impressions are made within fifteen seconds or less, and in that time people assume your social and economic status, educational level and the likelihood of your future success. Reversing an incorrect first impression can take up to five years.

When I was employed in a luxury goods company, I worked with a colleague who was not groomed professionally. It was not that he did not care—he simply lacked awareness. He was constantly the subject of many jokes and he had to work harder to prove himself. This situation was sad and unfair, yet proves once again that our appearance impacts our success at work.

Women who dress professionally are respected and taken seriously, while those who dress suggestively are not. There is no place for short skirts or low-cut blouses in the workplace. Jackets are a "no fail" article of clothing, because you are covered and "armed for business."

Men also need to pay attention to detail, even though they have less to risk given their limited clothing choices. Two dress issues for men are short ties and short pants. A man's tie should end at the bottom of his belt. A short tie that hangs above your belt conveys a lack of confidence. Pants should be long enough to hit the top of your back heel. Although these are small details, they convey confidence.

The Impact of Clothing in Business

In the workplace, we respond psychologically to colors, and each one conveys different messages. Use color strategically to convey your desired message.

- Black is dark and severe—a no nonsense color. Wearing a black suit portrays the person as important, the decision maker and the leader. This could be the CEO or president.
- Navy blue is the color of effectiveness and credibility. The British navy wore blue, and they were respected and committed. Wear a navy suit to chair a meeting or conduct interviews. Navy blue, as a color, compliments all complexions. Navy blue is a good choice for your first suit.
- Charcoal grey is also a color of trust and dependability. Charcoal grey is good to wear when attending to legal or financial matters, such as signing a contract.
- When you wear red, you will be remembered and also perceived as powerful and worth listening to. Red is a good color for a woman's power suit and a power tie for men. You and your message will be remembered longer.
- Burgundy is a color of maturity, and therefore a good choice for new college graduates who look young. Burgundy suggests refinement, maturity and experience.

When Hillary Clinton announced her candidacy for the U.S. Presidency, she wore a red jacket against a beige background. Her message was twofold. Her red jacket conveyed that she was a leader, a decision-maker and unafraid, while the softness of the beige background suggested approachability and friendliness.

Clothing Choices

Increasing your professional presence with a well-groomed image is not a recent phenomenon. As early as the 1830s, Ralph Waldo Emerson commented, "I have wondered how long men would retain their ranks if divested of their clothing."

Your clothing choices depend on your present position and the position to which you aspire. Here are the business dress levels starting with the most powerful.

Business Formal
Position—CEOs, vice presidents, senior executives
Men—Dark suit, white shirt, power tie and leather shoes with laces
Women—Dark skirt suit, hose and mid-heeled, closed-toe pumps
There is attention to details and grooming is impeccable. This look sends a message that the wearer is in charge, official and authoritative.

Business Classic
Position—Business owners, law, finance
Men—Matching suit with more flexibility of colors in the shirt and tie
Women—Matching pant suit
This visual conveys less formal authority, yet still sends a message of being in control.

Business Casual

This is the lowest level of dress and the cause of much confusion in the workplace. It is often referred to as Casual Confusion. It is important to remember at this level that business still comes first. This look is achieved with separate pieces rather than a matched suit. In particular, women should avoid sexy outfits that will sabotage their image in the business environment.

Workspace

Does your workspace look more like your living room than your professional space? Professional workspaces are always free of clutter and personal items. If you work with confidential information, ensure it is in a safe place while away from your desk. Rather than eating at your desk, take a well-deserved break by lunching elsewhere for socialization or a change of scenery.

Tidy your workplace before you leave for the day. Senior managers often stay late and the state of your work area will speak volumes about your work ethic.

If you are in the business of using your car to transport clients, its cleanliness reflects your attention to detail and consideration of them.

Advance with Professional Behavior

Punctuality. Be punctual. Lateness impedes the company's operations and is a tip that you are unreliable and not manager material. Conversely, do not arrive too early, as it is inconvenient when people are not ready for you. Be specific about the start and finish time when inviting people to meetings.

Effective meeting management. At Henry Ford's meetings, he insisted that only he had a seat and that everyone else should remain standing. This emphasized his control of the meeting and ensured they were brief and to the point. While such dramatics are unnecessary in today's professional environment, everyone appreciates the following:

• Successful meetings are brief, focused and productive.
• Start and end meetings on time.
• All electronics are turned off.
• End the meeting with action steps so that the meeting is productive.

Handshakes. In ancient times, handshakes were gestures of peace. Originally, the clasp was made on the forearm to ensure that no weapon was hidden in the sleeve. Over time, the greeting evolved into its modern form. It is the only type of acceptable touching in the business world.

• Never start a meeting without a handshake and good eye contact.
• In business, both men and women shake hands.
• Always stand up to shake someone's hand when you are introduced, and state your full name and position.
• Shake hands firmly with one squeeze. Your thumbs should meet web to web.

Appropriate Office Behavior

Some behaviors are of questionable taste and distract from your positive qualities. These include swearing and using terms of endearment with co-workers, telling sexist or racist jokes, and complaining about a co-worker, company or client. It is courteous to wash and return dishes you have used and make coffee if you take the last cup. Never reveal closely held company information, client confidences or salary levels. Be sensitive to the impact that important business information might have on those working on it or the competition—for example, a new product, a lay off or salaries.

While sharing with colleagues can be gratifying, avoid gossip because research has determined that less than one percent of the population can keep a secret. Gossip contributes to unproductive time, a loss of company money and has ruined the businesses and careers of many people. Be wary of people who gossip too much, as you could be associated with them or become a target of gossip yourself.

Office Party Etiquette—Eat, Drink and Be Wary!

Office parties can be fun and provide time to enjoy our colleagues in a different environment. They are also an opportunity to ruin or enhance your career. Even though it is a party, you will still be scrutinized about your attire, manners and body language. Here are some tips to ensure a good time while maintaining your professional etiquette.

- Greet upper management with a handshake and always address them professionally.
- Be aware of how much you eat and drink—no more than one or two drinks, since alcohol loosens inhibitions.
- Speak of general topics rather than "shop talk." It is wise to avoid controversial topics and to provide too much personal information.
- Use this opportunity to meet new people and avoid staying with your usual crowd for too long.
- Always say goodbye before you leave and thank the hosts for their kind hospitality.
- After the party, send a handwritten thank you note to the hosts. Since these are so rare today, your gesture will be remembered as a sign of good business manners.

Years ago, I attended a Christmas party and saw firsthand how inappropriate behavior can affect a person's life. A female employee danced all night in a very provocative way with a colleague, while her husband and the whole company watched. Her marriage ended shortly afterward and she never received the planned promotion that was to be offered to her in the new year.

Client Meeting at a Restaurant

Host. When you are the host at a client meeting, arrive at the restaurant early and inform the maitre d' that you will be paying. Give your credit card to the server to avoid confusion when the bill arrives.

Always confirm the appointment with your client the day before the meeting. As a courtesy to your client, select a restaurant close to her workplace. It is easiest for your guest if you wait at the front entrance for her. If there are more than two guests, waiting at the table is fine. Greet your guests just as you would in the office by standing and shaking hands before seating. When everyone arrives, put your napkin on your lap as a sign that you will begin. It is always best not to order alcohol. If your guest orders alcohol and asks that you have one, order one, however; you do not have to consume all of it.

Using Effective Communication

How we communicate. Albert Mehrabian, Professor Emeritus of Psychology at UCLA, conducted a study in 1981 on the effectiveness of three aspects of communication. The results of his research are astounding and are as follows:

• Verbal communication has an impact of 7 percent.

- Paralinguistic—sound and tone of voice and the way words are said—has an impact of 38 percent.
- Non-verbal behavior—body language and appearance—has an impact of 55 percent.

These results convey that people focus on your non-verbal communication rather than what you say, and emphasize the importance of professional appearance and confident body language.

Introductions. Knowing how to make proper introductions is important, both socially and in the workplace. In the business world, say first the name of the person to whom you want to show the greatest respect and honor. Customers always receive greater respect than anyone within the organization, even the CEO.

An example of an appropriate introduction might be: *Mr. Mitchell (client), I would like you to meet Ms. Bond, senior executive of the accounting department.*

Providing information about each person elicits conversation. For example, you could share that Ms. Bond transferred from the company's head office in New York.

In other situations, the easiest way to remember this rule is to introduce the most prominent person first, or the older person to the younger person or the woman to the man, followed by *"I would like you to meet."*

Also, be sure to stand up when making an introduction. By standing up, you convey the importance and respect of the individuals.

Business cards. Your business cards should appear professional and clearly state your relevant information. Ensure that you always have enough with you, and present them before a meeting begins. When someone gives you a business card, it is important to always look at the card before putting it away. This demonstrates an interest in the person and his or her business.

Telephone communication. It is important to maintain professionalism while speaking on the phone. Do not eat, drink or type on your computer. This behavior suggests that you are not attentive or respectful to what is being said.

Voicemail. Change your voicemail daily, stating the date and your availability. This extra effort is always appreciated.

- Always state your name, company and phone number at the beginning and your phone number again at the end, so the person has a second chance to record it.
- State your phone number slowly and clearly by stating a few numbers at a time.
- Keep messages brief when possible. Lengthy voicemails should be played back for accuracy.
- Never leave a negative or confidential message you may regret later. Recorded messages can be forwarded to others.
- If a long voicemail is necessary, organize your thoughts into points to allow a flowing message.
- Check your voicemail at least twice a day and return calls within 24 hours when possible.

Cell phones and text messaging. When communicating in person, refrain from texting at the same time. If you must take an important call during a meeting, inform the person ahead of time. If you are in a noisy place, explain to the person that it may be difficult to hear, however refrain from yelling. It may be best to call later when there are no distractions.

Email communication. Email is a quick and easy way to communicate. It is important to remember that once the information is in cyberspace, it is open for the world to view.

Here are a few things to keep in mind before pressing send:

- Always read your email before sending it.
- Writing in capitals is like shouting. You can get your point across by using other ways to highlight an idea.
- Limit your communication to business only, because your company can check your emails at any time.
- Use the person's name in the greeting and keep the email brief and concise. Bullet points are acceptable.
- If the message is too long, suggest a time to talk by phone.

Your Next Steps

When you consider the impact of practicing professional etiquette, the outcome is a win-win situation. Not only will people feel more comfortable in your presence, you will also be respected and considered as management material. Do not hesitate to take advantage of this simple, yet powerful tool.

Visit my website at www.lyndajean.com to request a complimentary consultation to help you achieve professional presence with ease.

Lynda Jean, MSW, AICI
Image Consultant, Corporate Speaker, Author

702-845-8369, Las Vegas
416-960-1333, Toronto
lynda@lyndajean.com
www.lyndajean.com

Lynda Jean is in the business of building confidence, transformation and supporting personalized goals for success. With a background in clinical social work and college instruction, Lynda brings compassion, wisdom and energy to her role as an image consultant and corporate speaker.

Lynda researched why certain people get the jobs, promotions and perks in life. She discovered that our non-verbal communication—our personal appearance and body language—accounts for 55 percent of how we are initially judged. Lynda's passion is to work with individuals and corporations to elevate their presence to a professional level. She works individually with clients to show them how to create powerful first impressions to become more confident and successful in their work.

She also delivers group presentations that address appropriate professional attire and etiquette in the workplace. Her empowering message encourages employees to make positive changes for themselves, which inevitably enhances both the corporate brand and their own career opportunities. Lynda has been an instructor at George Brown College in Toronto in the area of professional development and etiquette. She has been quoted on CNN®, has published articles and has appeared on Canadian television.

The Power of Intentional Networking with Ease

By Gloria L. Brown, CPPC

This chapter is going to change the way you think about the level of influence you leave in the room, whether you are attending a networking event, business meeting or just chatting with friends at dinner. The ability to influence others is powerful.

How many times have you realized that you need to meet more people or that your circle of influence needs to be strengthened? Networking has been proven to be one of the most powerful tools for helping you navigate your way to your ultimate goal. It is how you expand and grow a successful business with ease. Once the skill of networking is mastered, it can be used for any endeavor to accelerate success. Networking is an amazing vehicle for meeting and mingling with individuals, some of whom you might not have had a chance to speak with otherwise.

Intentional networking is entering a networking event or meeting with a strategic plan to purposely connect with people you would like to know more about. If your desire is to develop mutually beneficial relationships wherever you are, congratulations! You are an intentional networker. You are important to the success of others and the growth of their businesses.

Life is found in relationships with people, places and things. Thriving businesses are created by ideas and experiences. Infinite possibilities are fueled by these strong connections. These are then furthered by alliances with people who bring value and positive energy into our world.

Intentional networkers are those who show up with a positive attitude, energetic mindset, amazing skill sets, experience, vitality, purpose, values, business ethics, knowledge, talents, strength and enthusiasm. Networking simply means building relationships with others to learn, be of service or to teach, often all three. Meeting new people is a significant part of networking and so is learning from people you already know.

One of the best-kept secrets today is that businesses really do want to make a difference in the world and networking is a great way to make it happen. By activating what I call the *power principles* for networking and the generosity of sharing our authentic selves, we open doors for others. This helps people recognize their own intrinsic value so they can push past their limiting beliefs. This in turn allows them to develop successful strategies that will catapult their businesses to the next level.

The key to functioning effectively as *intentional networkers* is to master our connections with others: to gain knowledge and to be of service by igniting a spark that helps motivate people to learn, teach, move and grow.

Mindfulness, clarity, confidence and communication clear the way and open doors for growing your business with ease. These also enhance social standing, build excitement and confidence, as well as greater persistence, creativity and amazing performance. Powerful relationships are created when people recognize their greatest potential in their profound capability to change the world one person at a time. They do this by inspiring leadership, performance and growth—or what is also known as *influence.*

My experience as an expert strategist working with small businesses and sales people in large corporations, combined with my attendance at networking workshops, social gatherings and business events, has taught me one thing: For many, the common goal for networking is to connect, connect, connect. Their efforts are numbers driven; their goal is to gather as many business cards as possible from as many people as they can.

When asked, "Who would you like to connect with and why?" the answer tends to be ambiguous. These professionals usually have no idea. The power of intentional networking is to do your homework before engaging in a networking experience. Intentional networking is golden: successful people take positive steps to create dynamic, mutually beneficial relationships by bringing something of value to the table.

> *"We must be the change we wish to see in the world."*
> **—Mahatma Gandhi, father of the**
> **Indian independence movement**

Every day, many of us network from the comfort of our homes or offices. We spend a good part of our day participating in social media, posting on Facebook®, LinkedIn® and Twitter®. This leads to endless business opportunities and expands our reach to a global community. It is absolutely amazing. However, there is still something to be said about the human connection and the ritual of networking while fully engaged, whether it is face-to-face or voice-to-voice.

The power of being in a room with like-minded individuals is magical. The positive physical and emotional energy, firm handshakes and incredible smiles, wisdom, insight and brilliant ideas people bring into a room are powerful.

Be Authentic

There is nothing new under the sun and everything we do is merely a variation of a theme. It is important to activate your authentic self which differentiates you from anyone else. Motivation occurs from the desire to engage in activities because we value the inherent satisfaction it provides. Sharing yourself is a powerful way to influence others. Optimism is a powerful tool when networking on your journey to success. Networking to make an influential connection requires having a clearly defined sense of purpose and intent. Purpose is necessary to inspire mutually beneficial relationships. The model of *intentional networking* is based on the observation of highly effective professionals.

I have observed four common traits of effective networking.

1. The authentic self is the you that can be found at your absolute core. It is the part of you not defined by the roles you choose to play in life. It is the combination of all your skills, talents and wisdom. It is all of the things that are uniquely yours and need expression, rather than what you believe you are supposed to be and do. Be yourself at all times. Trust yourself. Know who you are and why. Conduct yourself in line with your core values and beliefs and remember actions speak louder than words.

Power of one. How many times have you attended a networking event and the first person you meet greets you with a smile? Then he hands you his business card and begins a scripted sales pitch for a product you have never heard of! No matter what you say, he does not stop talking. Then there is the arrogant network marketer—he has been in business for all of two days, tosses his business card in your face and proceeds to share how great he and his products are and why you need him now.

While these experiences can be extremely annoying, it is also a great opportunity to discover the power of intentional networking.

One expert can make a world of difference at a professional networking event. Remember, you are that expert. If it is additional information or skills a new contact needs, then point her in the right direction. If it is people this person needs to meet, offer an introduction or share other networking opportunities. Take every advantage to serve. Those who are new to networking have no idea how to maximize their connections. How they show up in a room is a strong indicator of how their networking efforts will influence others and the success of their business.

Have you ever noticed how some people connect in a room with ease, while others appear to be uncomfortable networking? Most of the time one's behavior has to do with fear of connecting with others. This comes from their perceived views of who is in the room and how they measure up. As the expert, it is important to help others feel at ease in the room. A successful networker is built by leveraging her strengths in a group. This is a powerful display of strong leadership skills.

2. Confidence, self-worth and the ability to communicate beyond your comfort level is key. How we measure up to others is not important. Empowerment is knowing your self-worth and how you can serve others. Using your great skills and knowledge is not only important to others, it also goes to the growth and success of your business.

"Although some people think that life is a battle,
it is actually a game of giving and receiving."
—Florence Scovill Shinn,
American philosopher and author

Intentional networking is a connection sport. There are many similarities between *intentional networking* and sports. Great athletes enter the arena with confidence, skills, focus, commitment and the intention of winning. What is your game plan? Who is on your team? Why are you in the room? There is no value in doing it alone just to prove you can. Focus on today. Why are you in the game?

Networking is a contact sport—you have got to touch somebody. The ability to motivate and influence others in business is connected to what we do today. The success of our business tomorrow depends on what we do today. Let me ask you, what can you do to win today?

John Wooden was the most successful college basketball coach who led the University of California, Los Angeles's team through ten National Championships in a twelve-year time span. In his philosophy, there was no reason not to play as hard in practice as any championship game. His message to every player was to go to bed each night thinking, *Today, I was at my best.*

Wooden also shared words of wisdom from his father, "Make each day your masterpiece." When learning a new skill or refining a technique, watch how successful people perform in the room. Expand your networking efforts by moving out of your comfort zone. Attend networking events you might not normally attend. The intent is to have a systematic approach to attract more clients, build your list and get more exposure. Sometimes you may have to regroup. Even so, always maintain your game face if you are not sure about the next move.

It is critical to make choices that will dramatically improve performance and help you discover which doors lead to endless opportunities for your business. *Intentional networking* can lead to new opportunities, mutually beneficial relationships, solid leads, web traffic and increased revenue.

3. Watch the professionals. Notice their posture and demeanor when they enter the room. Pay close attention to how people respond to them, how these professionals react to different environments and groups of people. You are observing the level of influence they have in the room. You can pick up valuable tips if you pay attention. Learn new strategies, develop your own style.

Wow—how did they do that? There is an old proverb that says, "Curiosity killed the cat." It was later amended to, "Curiosity may have killed the cat but satisfaction brought it back."

Good news! The cat is not dead. Curiosity is the desire to learn and discover. This desire to learn and discover has catapulted experts such as Dr. Oz, Deepak Chopra and many others to fame and fortune. In both cases, curiosity and *intentional networking* were the keys. Connecting with the right people at the right time and developing meaningful relationships with powerful people was key to the growth of their businesses. Now these people are considered curiosity experts. Their drive to explore new ideas and package old ideas in a different way often opens doors to endless business opportunities.

Intentional networking helps you develop powerful circles of like-minded, nurturing, positive and motivated people who believe in your vision, purpose and dream. This circle of influence represents the people who will open the door to the creation of wealth. People who respect, value and support your vision are your biggest fans. They express their belief in your ideas with conviction. Their recognition is the fuel that helps you grow and your business to thrive. They attend your workshops, webinars and retreats. Some will travel to wherever you are and they will refer others to experience, learn and enjoy the powerful programs and information you have created. Wow! You never know who is in the room.

4. Let your curiosity lead you to explore new and different ideas, dig deep for untapped resources, think outside the box and listen with an empathetic ear to find your hidden treasures. Consider packaging your incredible ideas, skills, education, background and experience into multiple sources of income. Learn to think outside the box.

THINKING OUTSIDE THE BOX

WHY am I here?

I've got
VALUE
to bring

I'm holding
the KEY to
my success!

I've GOT it!
There are
endless
opportunities
all over

---

*"You are your greatest asset. Put your time,
effort and money into training, grooming and encouraging
your greatest asset."*
**—Tom Hopkins, American founder of
Tom Hopkins™ International**

Be thirsty for knowledge and radical about your dreams, ideas and visions. Remember, curiosity is a major force behind science, research and other forms of human studies. Learn to market and package your incredible skills, education, background and experience. Connect with like-minded people and make it happen. There are no limits when it comes to the growth of your business.

Networking is both an art and a science. However, networking requires planning an approach that is intentional, strategic and measurable. Each time you introduce yourself to a new crowd or reacquaint yourself with an old one, learn what impact you had on the crowd. At the end of the day, networking should be fun, exciting and a rewarding approach to growing a thriving business with ease.

Here are some fun strategies to network with intention:

- Set goals to meet others in your field.
- Create a game plan for networking—know when, where, how much, how often. Be committed to achieving those targets.
- Understand why you are in the room. What is your niche?
- Great networkers want to know what they can do for you.
- A good conversationalist knows when to talk, what to say—and how to be a good listener.
- Have a memorable introduction that makes people want to know more about you.
- Join a networking group.
- Great networkers follow up within 24 hours. Send a handwritten thank you note. Use social media to stay connected with people.
- Unveil your passion.
- Ask for opportunities to assist when you see or hear of a need you can fill.
- Invite people to attend your events and workshops—this provides good exposure.

The right relationships can help you enter new markets, expand your services, sell more products, maximize exposure and increase revenue. For programs designed specifically for the ever-growing needs of your business or organization, sign up for my free newsletter on the Power of Intentional Networking at glospeaks2u.com.
Ready, Set, Grow!

Gloria L. Brown, CPPC
Vision Dynamic Motivational Institute
Creating Success Strategies for Intentional
Networking with Ease

510-967-6246
glospeaks2u@gmail.com
www.glospeaks2u.com

Gloria L. Brown is a highly sought after speaker, workshop facilitator, trainer, and Intentional Networking Strategist with more than 25 years of experience in the business and private sector. She uses powerful tools and techniques to deliver her message about intentional networking, "Ready, Set, Grow."

As a change agent, Gloria's strategies enable clients to take their "A" game into any room, any time. Her systematic approach targets personal and professional skill sets to create mutually beneficial relationships, no matter the circumstances. With an extensive background in sales and marketing and degrees in psychology, human development, behavioral science and women's studies, Gloria delivers high-energy, thought-provoking information for connecting and communicating with confidence and ease.

Gloria is the president of the East Bay Women's Network, where profound things happen as women connect with deeper meaning and intent. Her clients include The National Association of Educators, U.S. Environmental Protection Agency, Alameda County Office of Education, U.S. Department of Commerce, Alameda County Social Services, and the National Association of Educator/Teachers Association. Gloria's mantra is, *Where you are, you're supposed to be.* Now you can uncover additional insights for personal and professional growth by visiting Gloria at www.facebook.com/gloria.brown.399

Establish Your Digital Fingerprint with Ease

By Debbie Saviano

In my first career, I taught history. One of my favorite stories was of a newly married young pioneer wife living on the vast plains of Texas. Her husband was absent for long periods of time on trail rides. In her loneliness, she came up with the routine of tearing off tiny portions of her petticoat and writing notes which she tied to tumbleweeds and released to the wind. In her mind, she envisioned the "simple messages" being found and read by some other lonely woman on the prairie.

As they say, *We've come a long way, Baby!*

Not since the Renaissance in the 1400s with the invention of the printing press has there been such a revolution of information. The arrival of the Internet is upon us and is moving at lightning speed. Most would say, at full throttle. Daily tasks, events and actions are all reminders of the highly technical and digital world in which we are deeply immersed.

In this chapter, I will tell you how to manage life on the Internet—how to best establish your digital fingerprint—with ease.

Living in the Digital Age

- We are no longer tied or confined by boundaries and borders.
- Information is available 24/7.
- Users have global access to knowledge and information.
- The idea of "6 degrees of separation" has shrunk.
- The distinction between physical and virtual connectivity is blurred.
- Social media allows us to build relationships in a relaxed and personal manner.

Why is this important? Just as the demarcation between the physical and virtual is disappearing, so is the distinction between the personal and professional. When social media was first introduced, it was indeed possible to separate our lives into sections and categories. However, because of the rapid changes in technology, this is no longer true. In fact, our lives are all social and it is now a 24/7 engagement (see Diana Concoff Morgan's chapter, *Blogging Success with Ease,* on page 155). More and more shared platforms make it inevitable. Even when you are not physically present, your virtual representation is available. You might be asleep on the West Coast of the United States and yet in other parts of the world it is lunch time or even later. Your digital presence is always working!

> *"No one cares how much you know until they know*
> *how much you care."*
> **—Eleanor Roosevelt, former first lady of the United States,**
> **Civil Rights activist, philanthropist**

My approach to social media is always about the relationships. Growing up, I moved so many times I quit counting. Going to a new school two or three times a year was common. Unlike many of my friends, I enjoy meeting new people. Therefore, when embarking on any social media venture, it is with one goal in mind—developing, nurturing and maintaining relationships.

People do Business with People they Trust

Add to the above statement, those they "like." Think about it, do you engage in business with someone who is unkind, disloyal, dishonest or whom cannot be trusted? Feel confident the answer is no.

Consequently, the more you demonstrate an authentic, honest, transparent character, the more likely others will be drawn to you. Look around and notice how many people have a handheld device, a portal to citizens across the globe. Recent studies showed that forty percent of activity takes place on mobile instruments. Technology provides direct access to a worldwide audience and with each click, point or tap a story is told. Is it a drama, horror, comedy—or perhaps a documentary? A virtual identity is a story, and it is your story.

Normally, I do not use the pronoun "I" in my conversations, as I find the term "we" more powerful, inclusive and collaborative. However, in this case "I" will be the cornerstone of this chapter, so you can build your online presence with ease. Here is why the I's have it—they stand for: *Intention, Image, Information, Interaction, Influence and Involvement.*

Intentions and Your Virtual Identity

The Internet is the future, as is having a virtual or digital identity. A virtual identity is as real as a physical one and it behooves you to take an intentional approach to securing an identity that represents and reflects you today and in the future. Once information and images are on the Internet, they are always available. There is no delete button if the correct technology is available. Ask any investigator, hacker or tech guru. Once uploaded, it is almost impossible for content to be fully removed. Therefore, whatever you put up there should be a positive representation of you.

Images and Your Virtual Identity

Think about all the various social media platforms and venues available for interaction and engagement. Needless to say, the list is most likely quite long and constantly growing. The more involved you become with social media, the more avenues of interaction you have. When you join a new social media platform, it is important to take into consideration the value of clarity. Mostly, your goal is to complete the profile information and move on to the next task of the day. However, you must keep the long-range goal in mind. Think about the most recent social media site you joined. What was one of the first things you were encouraged to do? Upload an image.

Ask Yourself and Think About

• What is the first impression you wish to make?
• How would you like to be remembered?
• What is the mental image you want others to have of you?

When you answer the above questions, it is easy to understand the value of a consistent and professional image.

The What and Why of Headshots

A headshot is a picture used for branding. Naturally, the focus is on you and the intent is to portray your personality. There is a science and art to headshots. In most cases, one thinks of just the head. However, think more broadly and do some research.

• Google® the term *headshots*. Study the images and poses that speak to you.

• Is the person leaning in or sitting back? Are his hands shown? Is her head tilted? Is he flashing a full smile or just a partial one? Is the image in color or black and white?

• Tell the photographer which pose, angle and lighting you prefer.

• Let me tell you how important it is to have what I call "crisp eye shots." This is when the person in the photo appears to be meeting your own gaze straight-on. Eyes are considered the "windows to the soul" and draw in the viewer.

• Distinguish yourself by using a non-air brushed photo.

• Regardless of when or how someone meets you, it is paramount to be recognized.

• First impressions are lasting and therefore, it is important to make sure yours is positive, memorable and consistent with your professional image.

• Use the same headshot for all your social media images.

Information and Your Virtual Identity

You have an image that is reflective of your personality. Now it is time to consider the message and the information which identifies you. Again, think about the social media platforms where you are present. Have you created a uniform message communicating the solutions, values, belief system, ideals, statistics, product or service you provide? Enduring images and information help regulate the success of you and your business.

Ask yourself and think about:
- What information defines and is unique to you?
- You have heard it before—who is your ideal client?
- What are the ten to fifteen keywords that describe your product, idea or service.
- How can the information be condensed into three sentences?
- Guarantee that your online message is congruent with your business offline.

Taking time to identify your message verifies who you are, your value system, how you are unique, the solutions you offer. Once you have clarity, this is the information that needs to be included on all social media platforms, from your bio to your headlines. Providing the information and details enables the digital world to rank, classify and find you.

Interactions and Your Virtual Identity

You now have a professional image, with information reflective of you and your business. Now it is time to interact. It is called social media for a reason. Communication involves sharing, imparting and exchanging information. Remember, information and images online are timeless and permanent in that it is almost impossible to ever fully remove something once you post it. Hitting delete only removes it from those people without the necessary tools or skills to retrieve it.

It is never too early to begin considering your digital identity and having a well thought-out plan for interaction. Always maintain a professional mode, the image you want others to see.

Ask yourself and think about:

• Which social media platforms are my ideal clients using?
• How will my interactions online maximize engagement?
• Adopting a philosophy for positive interaction is necessary.
• Interactions online are simply digital conversations and the same courtesy and respect that you give to a live conversation is needed.
• What topics can I address to build a community and inspire others?

Influence and Your Virtual Identity

The traditional definition of ROI is *return on investment*. Today, it refers to *influence*. Being viewed as an influencer, an expert in the industry, affects the viewpoint, perception and actions of those you wish to attract, help, serve and do business with.

If done correctly, the social connections and networking you do ultimately leads to influence, which in turn leads to success.

Ask yourself and think about:

• Make the interactions personal and with purpose.
• Being present on a consistent basis produces trust.
• Always keep a business mindset.
• Consider that there is no longer a separation of your personal and professional personality.
• The more active you are, the more opportunities for engagement.

Involvement and Your Virtual Identity

As I mentioned, being present with a clear, consistent image and message increases influence. What is also significant to remember is the vast amount of choices you have when doing business. The more positive and comprehensive your information, the more likely your business will succeed. Visualize all the social media places where you are involved. This online real estate provides the opportunity to leverage all the communication taking place. There are countless places where people go to hang out. These six are recognized as the "Big Players."

1. LinkedIn®

2. Facebook®

3. Twitter®

4. Pinterest®

5. Google® +

6. You Tube®

Presence and Activity on Social Media are a Given

Your customers are hanging out online. That means being visible in this virtual world, doing business in this online marketplace, is not an option.

Your virtual representation can either be homogeneous, meaning there is a clear and consistent portrayal of who you are, or one that is disjointed, confusing and inconsistent. Needless to say, we seek to have a crystal clear depiction of who we are. When done correctly a transparent, trusted picture develops.

Social media users vary and there is plenty of data and statistics available as to when and where certain activities take place online.

For our purposes here, let us focus on establishing an online presence with the site that has the highest number of professionals—LinkedIn.

LinkedIn is a professional virtual rolodex. With more than 200 million users worldwide and an average household income of $100,000, the usefulness of LinkedIn is non-debatable. What makes LinkedIn unique is the emphasis on the professional user.

• LinkedIn users are in a business mindset.
• Every industry and profession is represented.
• Conversations and discussion vary, yet even in the causal groups each person participating is a professional.
• International audiences use LinkedIn.
• Influencers, thought leaders, clients and prospects are present.

Six Ways to Use LinkedIn with Ease

1. Your professional image is paramount.

2. Your headline needs to speak directly to your target client, audience and visitor.

3. The Summary section has 2,000 characters—use it to your advantage. Share an overview of who you are and why you are the best choice to do business with.

4. Having accurate and up to date contact information is critical. Including it in the summary section guarantees the visitor can contact you.

5. Talk to your ideal client throughout the profile. Think of the person you wish to attract as a visitor to your profile. With each word you write ask yourself, *Will this keep the visitor engaged on my profile?* Write for the skimming eye, that means use shorter sentences, bullet points, white space and use of icons to draw attention.

6. Real estate equals valuable space. Take the time to completely fill out your LinkedIn profile. It is how you showcase your expertise and confirm you are the best choice to do business with.

Five More Easy Ways to Use LinkedIn

1. Activity—post content, promote other valuable content

2. Produce new content—white papers, infographics, videos

3. Promote—give endorsements and write recommendations for people you have done business with

4. Network—invite people to connect with you, respond to invitations and questions you are asked, form a personal relationship

5. Participate—get involved in group discussions

Ask Yourself and Think About:
- The image and message should be uniform.
- It is important for your personal and professional information to positively reflect on your business image and reputation.
- Virtual information can have consequences on how you are perceived as they might not have met you in person. Therefore, it is important to insure it is a positive reflection of your professional skills and expertise.
- Social media platforms enable you to continue the conversation.

- Use social media as a conduit to increase exposure for your own website.
- Complete your entire LinkedIn profile, including the Bio, About and Summary sections.

As the Internet expands and the number of users increases, you have additional opportunities to network, establish your credibility, keep your current clients informed, build a community and hopefully, gain new clients. As you create your virtual identity, ensure your online image is a direct reflection of your offline business. Generate an online presence reflective of you and your business.

When you interact and engage online, remember the aforementioned "I's." By implementing *Intentions, Images, Information, Interaction, Influence and Involvement,* you will establish your digital fingerprint with ease.

Debbie Saviano
Life is a banquet, and if we choose, we have a seat at the table.

214-707-2195
debbie@debbiesaviano.com
www.debbiesaviano.com

Debbie Saviano spends her time helping professionals take action and create an online presence by developing, nurturing and maintaining relationships. As a social media strategist, speaker and a champion for building relationships, Debbie is an advocate for continuing the conversation and places high value on building relationships.

With a background in education and a degree in English, history and psychology, Debbie implements a practical approach to social media. Professionals choose Debbie for her distinct skill set in designing LinkedIn and Pinterest accounts. Speaking and training enable Debbie to remain close to those interested in continuing to learn and embrace technology as well as discovering innovative methods to build relationships.

Debbie has served her community through the Junior League and numerous other volunteer programs. In 2012, she was honored with an Innovative Women in Business award. She was also selected as one of fifty women from across the country to participate in the national program of Leadership America. In 2013, Interesting Talks London invited Debbie to speak at their event, allowing Debbie to build her relationships and reach across the Atlantic. Next up: Debbie travels to India as part of an International Leadership Program.

Blogging Success with Ease

How to be seen, create whole heart connections and attract more clients

By Diana Concoff Morgan, MA, HHE

This chapter is about how you can successfully create and grow your online presence with ease through blogging. The goal of this chapter is to show you how to attract your customers to your site and create a relationship with them, so that when they are ready to buy, you are the one they want to buy from. There is so much information available about how to be successful with your Internet marketing. It can be confusing to know exactly where to focus your efforts. Creating a *whole heart* connection is a proven strategy you can use to be seen, get known and attract more clients. It is your whole heart connection that makes the difference!

The whole heart connection is the connection you make with your online following to the part of you who cares, the expert in you, the committed, dedicated you. When you bring your *whole heart* to your online presence, your client feels you, she connects with you, she knows you care about her and she begins to feel like she knows and trusts you. This is the beginning of creating an authentic relationship with your client.

Currently there are more than two billion users of the Internet. I like to describe the Internet as a 24/7 networking opportunity (see Debbie Saviano's chapter, *Establish Your Digital Fingerprint with Ease,* on page 143). When you are at a live, in-person networking event, you walk up to a person, introduce yourself, shake hands and start chatting about your business and other things. Because you are a savvy networker, you probably introduce the person you just met to other people in the room you know and that person does the same for you. That is how your network grows—you create connections that turn into relationships and you gain business influence.

The biggest difference between how you connect with another person at a live, in-person networking event and how you connect on the Internet is how the connection is made. At the networking event, the connection is a handshake. On the Internet, the "handshake" is made via a hyperlink (the hyperlink is the link you click on to get from one place on the Internet to another). You refer your connections to one another on the Internet via the links that are found on sites like Facebook®, Twitter®, LinkedIn®, Google®+, YouTube®, Pinterest®, Flickr® and all the other social networks, online directories, social bookmarking sites, websites and blogs.

A few examples of how this works would be the connections you create on Facebook when you like, comment, share and tag people. If you are on Twitter, it is when you "re-tweet" something that has been "tweeted" previously. These are Internet referrals that create inbound links to your website or blog (inbound links are the links that bring visitors to your site from another site on the Internet). Another example would be if you post the link to your blog on Facebook and then people share your blog posts on their page or someone else's page or in a group. The beautiful thing about the Internet is that these networking opportunities are available 24/7. In fact, every twenty minutes more than one million links are exchanged on the Internet—that is more than a million "Internet handshakes" or referrals!

Social media sites may come and go, however the foundation of the Internet will always be based on sharing quality content—information—via links.

Here is How You Can Get More of those Links Referring You!

Blogging for your business is one of the top strategies you can use to market your business on the Internet because it offers endless opportunities to make authentic connections, build relationships and encourage referrals. A business blog is different from a hobby blog. There are free hobby blog sites like WordPress.com and Blogger. com. What you actually have on these sites is a blog on someone else's website. The problem with this is that you do not have control of your online presence. You do not own your content. You do not have your own domain name. Sometimes blogs are deleted from these sites and you have no control over that, either.

For your *business blog,* I recommend setting up your blog as a website and using a WordPressTM template. You can get a template for free at www.wordpress.org and then upload it to your website. WordPressTM is a blogging platform that was created to be found easily by the search engines. It offers lots of free tools to improve your online search results. By having your blog on your own website, you have complete ownership of your content and your domain name and you have complete control over your blog. The set-up is fairly easy to do and very inexpensive.

Get Links Through Social Media

A business blog has a strategic focus related to your marketing message. You can share your blog posts on Facebook, LinkedIn, Twitter and other social media. People can then share or re-tweet your blog posts. When people share your blog, this positions you as the expert in your field. People can comment on your blog and then share their comments and your blog post on social media. Every time your blog is shared, you have a new opportunity to come up in Google search results. Guess what—your blog posts live on the Internet forever. Each individual blog post has its own address on the Internet linking back to your site.

You Can Use Your Newsletter to Share Your Blog

A blog and a newsletter are not the same. Your newsletter has time-sensitive content such as workshop dates, upcoming events, special promotions and information about your business. You can create blog posts about these types of things for your blog, however you want to have "evergreen" articles as well. Evergreen means that the article is not time-sensitive. It will still be relevant in a year or two.

You can share a "snippet" of each of your blog posts in your newsletter with a link to your blog on your website. This will encourage your newsletter readers to go to your website to see your blog and they will also see all the other great offerings you have on your website.

You Can Guest Blog to Increase Your Influence

Guest blogging is another powerful way to create influence and position yourself as an expert on the Internet. You can invite guest bloggers to your blog and you can blog on other peoples' blogs. Think about people who would be strategic partners for you. As strategic partners, you each have different services or products to offer the same or a similar market. You can create blog posts on each other's blogs, thus increasing your market and influence. To find strategic partners' blogs, search the Internet by typing into Google keywords related to your strategic partners followed by the word blogs. For example, if a business coach is a strategic partner for you, type the words *business coach blogs* into Google.

Whether as a guest blogger yourself or having a guest blogger on our own site, you want fresh, new content. The search engines prefer that content not be exactly the same in more than a couple of places. Even if you know someone who does not blog, you can still invite them to write a post for you. If they have an email list, you can ask them to share your blog with the people on their email list. Guest blogging is a powerful way to increase traffic and expert status.

Where to Create *Whole Heart* Connections with Your Readers

Share Your Blog. You can submit your evergreen articles to article marketing sites online. Most of these sites require article length to be between 375 and 500 words and have no more than two or three hyperlinks in the article. Feel free to write your promotional posts and personal posts on your blog along with some articles as well. Then you can share your articles on other article sites.

Search out relevant sites on the Internet where you can post your articles and include links back to your site. Popular sites include www.ezinearticles.com and www.isnare.com. To find more sites, type the words *article marketing sites* into Google. You can also use your keywords to search for article sites. For example, if one of your keywords is *allergy,* you would type *allergy articles* into Google.

Join blogs that are related to your topic and participate using your signature box to link back to your site. The signature box allows you to enter your website address. There are a few blogs that do not allow you to have a signature link, therefore choose the ones that do allow it.

Join groups on LinkedIn and Facebook. You can find relevant groups by searching your keywords in the search bar on these sites. Participate actively in the groups that you join. Be helpful—95 percent information, 5 percent promotion.

Whether it is blogs, forums or article sites, find the most popular, active sites that are relevant to your potential clients. The most active sites have current content posted. By contributing content to these sites, you will be increasing traffic to your site. Your customers will find you because you have more content on the Internet and your content will be linked to your site either through the signature box or through your keywords.

Blogging gives you a way to keep in touch with your potential clients. You can continue to provide them valuable, quality information and then when they are ready to buy, you are the one they choose because you are the one who has been there consistently, building the relationship, sharing your heart and providing quality information. You are the one they know, like and trust!

The Formula for Creating Whole Heart Connections

There will always be a new social networking site, like Facebook or Twitter—a new place to hang your "virtual shingle." What will never change is how important it is that you offer really great, useful information and a way for people to connect with you from the heart so they keep coming back for more.

Write from your heart to your client's heart. Choose an imaginary or real client. Become your client, open to knowing her thoughts. Speak to her as you write your posts. Show her that you get her—make her feel known and understood. Make sure your content is relevant to your client. For example, if you are a photographer, your content might be about how to be a good photographer or how to look better in photos. Become the resource for the most current tips and strategies in your industry. Share relevant and inspirational stories relating to your experience. They can be personal or professional. The more you share of yourself in your blog, the more people will be able to connect with you.

Ideas for Creating a *Whole Heart Connection:*

- Share stories and personal experience.
- Offer examples of ways that you have helped your clients and how you worked with them.
- Be real, show your personality.
- Share your experience—getting a little personal is okay.
- Combine useful information with a personal tone.
- Encourage conversation from your readers by inviting opinions, questions or comments.
- Engage your readers with polls, questionnaires and surveys.

Share solutions. Make a connection with your readers by expressing what you believe their challenges are. Address those challenges in your content by offering solutions.

Engage your reader by answering her questions. As you write your posts, imagine your ideal client; think about what questions she might be asking. Ask yourself, *What does she need to know that she isn't even asking?*

Your reader wants to know about you and your work with your clients. Share client success stories. Unless there is a confidentiality issue, it is a good idea to use real names and link to their websites. Client testimonials are powerful. When you give your reader useful information, including solutions, you stand out in the sea of bloggers. You are the one she remembers because she feels you, she connects with you.

Your reader wants content that is easy to read. Keep in mind, she is so busy and overwhelmed with her life and her business that she will tend to gravitate toward content that is easier to read. I recommend using very down-to-earth language. Remember that there is so much content on the Internet, you want her to read your content because she feels like you are talking directly to her.

Use your keywords. Include your keyword phrases in your content, once or twice in a paragraph at the most. These days, less is more, therefore make sure you do not overdo it on the keywords. Your keyword phrases are the words your customer would use to search for you on the Internet. Keep in mind that your client is going to search for you by describing her problem. She does not know the solution you have to offer her! Therefore, your keywords will be words that describe your client's problem.

I invite you to stay current with the latest trends in search engine optimization by subscribing to my *Whole Heart Marketing Report.* In it, I share current, non-techy strategies for successful Internet marketing. There is a link to sign up at the end of this chapter.

Keep the conversation going. Consistent and frequent participation creates momentum. When you regularly post content, your readers expect it and look forward to it. In addition, every time you post new content, your content is indexed—included in search results—by Google and other search engines. This means your content is available to your customers and you appear higher up in the search engines when they search for your product or service.

The more you post quality content, whether in the form of blogs and articles or social media, the more you appear as an expert in your field to *your* customers.

Keep message consistency in mind. You want your message to be consistent throughout your online presence so people start to recognize you, whether it is your website, blog or social media. That is part of building the relationship. I encourage you to have one focused message for your blog and then make sure all topics are related to that message. You can have as many blogs as you would like to have, however keep the message consistent and the topics related to the message on each blog.

If you have a couple of related topics that you blog about, you can have them on the same blog, however I recommend blogging about the same topic for ten posts and then you can switch to another topic.

Whole Heart Marketing
Triple Win Blogging Challenge

I invite you to join in the *Whole Heart Marketing Triple Win Blogging Challenge*. We have a Facebook group you can join. This is an on-going challenge. You can join any time. Here is how it works:

- Three blog posts per week
- Three shares of other peoples' blogs
- Three comments on other peoples' blogs
- Do this for thirty days. Hopefully you will continue on after the first thirty days are up.

Here is the *Triple Win!* Your clients win because they get great information from you. You win because you get more influence and attract more clients for your business with ease. The Internet wins because we are all putting out great, useful content. This upgrades the quality of the Internet and helps us create community through our whole heart connections!

Sign up for the *Whole Heart Marketing Report* today at www.wholeheartmarkteting.com!

Diana Concoff Morgan, MA, HHE
Whole Heart Marketing

925-980-9052
diana@wholeheartmarketing.com
www.wholeheartmarketing.com

Diana Concoff Morgan, MA, HHE, CEO of Whole Heart Marketing is a speaker, author, trainer, successful entrepreneur and certified coach specializing in Internet marketing, blogging, social media and SEO. Her mission is to help entrepreneurs crack the Internet marketing code with hands-on help and simple strategies to be seen, create whole heart connections, get known and attract more clients. She will teach you, coach you or do it for you.

Diana's results-oriented strategies have helped countless entrepreneurs get found by their clients in Google searches. She makes the Internet a user-friendly place. Diana succeeded in creating a nondenominational wedding ministry that performed more than 100 weddings a year with six trained ministers, becoming one of the most successful, professional full-time ministries in the San Francisco Bay Area through her online and offline marketing expertise.

She serves on two boards: One is Connections, A Forum for Women. This is a non-profit organization that raises money for "at risk" girls and women re-entering the work force. The other is The Enchanted Business Woman, a professional networking association. Diana lives in Santa Rosa, California with her husband of 25 years and their cat, Fluffy.

Marketing Your Services on eBay® with Ease

How to open your business to the world

By Danni Ackerman

Many people know eBay as an online marketplace to sell your grandmother's old dishes, your children's outgrown clothing, or even a car. However did you know you can sell services there also? It is true! You can tap into a huge resource of potential customers by setting up an eBay store. There are a lot of things you may not have thought about when it comes to marketable products for your business. Let me show you how you can effectively utilize eBay as another tool in your business's marketing toolbox.

eBay has over one million active registered users. That number continues to grow. eBay is not going anywhere and is getting a stronger hold in the eCommerce community by the day. There are billions of listings created on eBay each year and only a very small percentage of them are service-based listings. What this means for you is a tremendous opportunity to tap into the eBay highway to promote your business.

How Do I Get Started on eBay?

If you have only heard about eBay, yet never actually explored it, I can assure you it is very user friendly and easy to get set up on. You may already have an account on eBay, yet only used it for buying stuff. Setting up a selling account is really an easy process that takes just a few minutes.

Here is what you need to do:

- **Go to eBay.com** and in the upper left hand corner you will see a place to sign in or register. This opens up into a very easy-to-fill-out form that includes information such as your name, email address and the user ID you choose. Once you have created your account, you can set up a selling account by clicking the Sell button in the top left corner. This requires setting up a PayPal® account so you can accept payments.
- **Listing your first item.** Getting started is as easy as listing your first item on eBay. You will be prompted to enter all the information you need on the sell your item form. They have made the whole process fairly user-friendly. There is even a listing form that is just for those getting started and is super easy to follow.
- **eBay has a category just for you.** eBay has a category for specialty services. Within this main category are several sub-categories to choose from and you can narrow down to the one that fits your service best.

Tips for Building Your eBay Business

eBay goes by a feedback system that lets potential customers know some information about you. From this feedback profile, a person can see how long you have been registered on eBay, where you are located and your reputation as an eBay buyer and seller. A first goal should be to reach a score of ten on feedback received. It seems that the number ten is a magic number and customers start trusting you more and feeling comfortable buying from you. Here are some things you can do to build your eBay reputation faster:

- Make some purchases on eBay. This helps you accumulate your first ten feedback reviews more quickly.
- When making a sale, be sure and leave feedback for your customer as soon as payment is received.
- Always be responsive to customers and potential customers to get the best feedback possible. Good customer service is a must for building a solid eBay reputation.

Remember the eBay system is built around seller reputation. They have a program called the Top Rated Seller Program. When attained, this will give you a higher search rank, as well as discounts on the fees charged when someone makes a purchase from you. In order to attain the Top Rated Seller status you must meet the following requirements:

- Have an eBay account that has been active for at least ninety days.
- Have a positive feedback rating of at least 98 percent.
- Have at least 100 transactions and $1,000 in sales with U.S. buyers over the most recent 12-month period.
- Upload shipment tracking details to your buyers within your promised handling time for at least 90 percent of your transactions with U.S. buyers in any 3-month period. Shipment tracking is the signature confirmation number provided by USPS® or the tracking number provided by UPS® or FedEx®.

One of the hardest parts in getting an eBay business up and running is building up the feedback score to reflect you are not just someone who dropped in to take a customer's money and run. You are a solid account holder.

There are a few other requirements I should mention as well. eBay has a rating system called the Detailed Seller Ratings or DSR's. Buyers can rate a seller in four categories at the same time they leave feedback.

1. Item as described

2. Communication

3. Shipping time

4. Shipping and handling charges

To achieve and maintain the Top Rated Seller status, you cannot get more than two low ratings—a one or a two—in any of the four categories and a one-half percent of your total transactions. In other words, it takes both the maximum number of two plus the one-half percent of your transactions to make you *ineligible* for the TRS status.

Do not get scared off by all these numbers. I assure you most sellers do just fine by following good customer service practices, which I am sure is already part of your business.

Some Rules About Service-Related Products

eBay has some fairly stringent rules when it comes to selling your service-related products on its site. It is important to become familiar with them because the last thing you want is to be shut down before you ever really get started! Here are some examples of what is not allowed:

• Personal advice and coaching
• Website traffic-driving services, search placement services and banner ad services
• Offers for personal relationships of any kind, including through social networking sites like Facebook®

The key is to have a tangible product. Even in the case of eBooks, you must mail out the actual disc (CD) containing the eBook, even if you deliver it electronically as well. This rule was put in place a few years ago to prevent the fraud that was becoming prevalent in this category.

Some ideas for service-related businesses include:

- An informational eBook or pamphlet you can mail out on a CD as well as electronically
- Tickets to a live event you may be holding
- A workbook to go along with a workshop or virtual training session you are holding
- A gift certificate for services you provide—it is okay if the gift certificate is for coaching

As you can see, the idea here is to have a product you can prove you delivered to the customer. While you may be using eBay as a way to provide more intangible services such as coaching or consulting, if you follow these tips you will avoid getting into trouble with eBay—and possibly having your account suspended.

What is it Going to Cost Me?

You may be wondering what the cost of bringing your business to eBay will be. I assure you it is extremely reasonable! There are two types of fees you will be responsible for—insertion fees and final value fees.

Insertion fees are charged when you create a listing. There are different levels of this fee depending on whether or not you have an eBay store and what level of store you have. If you do not have an eBay store, you get fifty free listings each month. After that you pay thirty cents per listing. For the basic store level, you get one-hundred-fifty free store listings. Once you reach that level, you pay twenty cents per listing.

If your goal is to stick strictly to service-based products, and you want to use your eBay store as a way to drive traffic to your main website, a basic store is perfect for you. You will probably never experience insertion fees.

Final value fees, also known as FVF, are the fees you are charged when a product sells. The amount you pay is based on what your customer pays, including shipping and handling costs. If your item does not sell, you are not charged an FVF. For sellers who do not have a store subscription, the FVF is 10 percent of the total sale, up to $250 maximum.

For sellers who have an eBay store subscription, it works a little differently. The basic store subscription is $19.95 per month. If you commit to a full year, it goes down to $15.95 per month. If you go over your 150 free listings per month, then an insertion fee of twenty to twenty-five cents per unit will apply. The FVF for store owners goes down to 9 percent.

Why Would I Want to Open an eBay Store?

I am often asked by new sellers on eBay, "Why should I open a store on eBay?" An eBay store is chock full of amazing marketing tools and search engine optimization features—it is incredible they have not raised their prices to reflect the value they are offering. Here are just some of the things an eBay Store can do for your business:

• **Store home page and unlimited product pages.** This is a place for you to create and build your brand or expand on the one you already have outside of eBay. You can pick your colors, logo and even your store categories.

- **You get custom pages.** These are customizable pages to boost your brand, communicate store policies, and connect with customers. This is the equivalent of fifteen mini websites.
- **Customized web address.** You will get your very own URL, therefore you can drive buyers directly to your store.
- **Promotion boxes.** These are places to highlight premium merchandise in your store to trigger sales. You can also use a promotion box to build an eBay store newsletter. This is how your repeat customers can hear from you regularly.
- **Custom store header.** You can create a customized, branded header with merchandising and keywords to drive more traffic to you.
- **There are tools for marketing as well as tools to track your success.** eBay provides a way to keep all your eBay information in one place and manage your store. There are templates and promotional flyers available for you to create and use. Traffic and sales reports will help you know who is finding your eBay store and narrow it down to the very path they took to get there.

You can now see the enormous value and potential an eBay store has for growing your business. It is a site that Google® pays a lot of attention to and having your service-based business on eBay will play a big part in being found within those Google searches.

The Keys to Having eBay Expand Your Brand

With any business, there is a need to constantly acquire new customers and clients. eBay spends hundreds of thousands of dollars to keep its brand in front of the public eye as well as expand into new marketplaces. If you have the type of service-based product that customers can buy from all over the globe, eBay is the perfect spot. Even if you can only provide services locally, eBay is probably in the favorites list of hundreds of your potential customers right in your own town. Consulting and coaching can all be done virtually these days, why not offer these services to buyers all over the country?

Here are some recommendations for taking your business onto eBay:

- Be consistent with your colors, logo and theme
- Take time to write up a professional, keyword-rich listing
- Take advantage of all the marketing tools eBay has to offer

While I am sure you are utilizing other aspects of marketing—such as social media sites—sometimes people are more comfortable getting to know you through a well-known venue such as eBay. They know they have protections in place should you not live up to their expectations. Keep in mind once the transaction has been completed, this is now your customer. When they pay through PayPal, you are provided with a receipt that has their email address and other information included. Keep this information safe, however do not use it right away. Let your customer receive the product she requested. Once you deliver it, now you can give her ways to connect with you further. Be sure to clearly provide your contact information both in correspondence with her as well as in the package you send out. eBay works to prevent sellers from contacting buyers by any means other than through its messaging system. Be respectful of this rule in order to stay out of trouble.

One last caution—never put your email address or link to an outside website within your eBay listings! This is a big no-no and can get you suspended from the site. That is the bad news. The good news is you can include outside links in other places within your eBay store, like your About Me page. This is where customers go to learn more about you and your business.

Now it is Time to Reap the Rewards!

If you have the type of service-based product that brings customers to you from all over the globe, eBay is the perfect way to build a new online business with ease. By turning your intangible consulting and coaching services into a tangible, mail-ready product, you can extend your reach, your reputation and your revenue. Play by the rules and stay true to your brand and you will carry your message to a whole new world of clients.

I love helping others find their success on the eBay marketplace! To receive ongoing information and opportunities for selling your services on eBay, visit www.whatdoyousell.com.

Danni Ackerman

Founder and Chief Inspiration Officer

The Danni App for Fun...and Profit!

702-425-4115

danni@thedanniapp.com

www.thedanniapp.com

Since 1998, Danni has been an ecommerce seller working her way up from hobby selling to supporting her family during rough times. Her passion is selling on eBay where she has sold nearly a quarter of a million dollars in antiques and collectibles.

Today, Danni not only continues to operate a successful eBay business—she is also reaching out to share her years of experience with others through virtual training and speaking engagements around the country. Danni is the author of the *For Fun and Profit Series* where she teaches others how to find treasures to resell. She is also the co-author of *The Ultimate Guide to Savings by Store.*

Her experience goes back to a childhood spent working in an antique store and thrift shop alongside her aunt. Danni has brought her mom and daughters into the business and is now part of a three-generation ecommerce family. Danni has figured out how to juggle business and home life successfully and teaches others to do the same.

Using Events as a Marketing Strategy to Grow Your Business with Ease

By Linda Cain

Have you considered using live events as part of your marketing strategy to grow your business? If not, you are missing out on one of the greatest opportunities to connect face-to-face with your current client base, as well as potential clients. Holding events as part of your marketing strategy will help increase your visibility and improve your sales.

Attending other industry events will give you a chance to scope out the competition, allow you to gather information on their strengths and weaknesses and conduct research that will give your business a cutting edge.

Everyone is pretty much aware of low-cost and high-cost online marketing strategies, such as webinars, teleseminars, telecasts, live streams and more; however there is no substitute for live, in-person opportunities to gain visibility, build relationships and set you up as the expert.

Live events have become the best way to create a unique experience for your audience. Whether it is a one-, two- or three-day event, you are creating the perfect opportunity to showcase your expertise. This allows you to educate and connect with colleagues, industry leaders and fellow entrepreneurs. Providing a place for people to connect, learn and grow deepens and enhances relationships and bonds them even further to you.

The objective is to create an experience that is so engaging and relevant to your business that participants talk about it on social media, post photos and create consistent buzz about you. Live events where people can feel, touch and experience you deepens the relationship, something that cannot easily be done by simply reading your blogs, listening to your audios and watching your videos.

As you may know, just after 9/11, the meeting and trade show industry made major cutbacks and some firms and individuals quit going to trade shows and attending or holding meetings altogether. However, something else that happened was that the people who used to go to these events just to go, quit going. They simply disappeared in our new economy.

What does this mean and why does it matter to you and your next event? Growth in live event marketing is growing faster than the economy, from 3.6 percent in 2011 to 7.8 percent in 2012 and continuing upward in 2013. The recession basically got rid of all the window shoppers. Now we have people—entrepreneurs or company representatives—who attend events because they are looking to grow their skills or business. They are actively looking to invest and have the resources to do so.

This is great news for those of us who want to make live events part of our marketing strategy to grow our business!

Still wondering if hosting a live event is right for you? Here are five ways holding a live event will grow your business:

1. Positions you as the authority and elevates your brand. You gain huge credibility and visibility by hosting your own live event. It helps you build an amazing community around you. Producing your own event is a way to design your own network and strengthen ties with other key players in your field. This means your reputation can be fueled by the buzz created at the event. Add in your own genuine style and relationship with your audience and you will have a band of loyal followers begging for more.

Following your live event, you can offer your mastermind programs, continuing education programs, ongoing seminars, workshops and teleclasses to a growing audience of great supporters and potential clients.

2. Boosts creativity and innovation. Holding your own live event is a great platform for sharing the latest techniques and innovations that will improve your audience member's businesses. Studies have proven that taking a break from the day-to-day operations of one's business, getting a change of scenery—especially one that is rich with networking and educational opportunities—is highly beneficial to your audience.

The best advantage: The tremendous opportunity for you to create more content, more programs, more upsells—more ways for you to connect with your audience and grow your own business.

Giving your clients practical skills and tools to help them grow their businesses in a live event environment keeps them coming back to you over and over again.

3. Brings together community that knows, trusts, likes and buys. It is no big secret that people do business and purchase programs from people they know, trust and like.

Holding your own live event provides the best platform to have a captive audience that is there to listen and experience what you have to say. Providing great content and setting the stage for your audience to have an amazing experience will create a loyal community.

4. Generates strategic alliances. Design a program that allows speakers and sponsors to become strategic partners with you. This helps reduce the cost of hosting your event. Your partners also can help market and promote your event among their own customers, thus expanding your reach. Teaming up gives you more marketing power, and because your strategic partners are also promoting your event, you save money on additional advertising costs.

To encourage sponsors to spread the word, you can sweeten the deal by providing a promotional package, including pre-written emails, social media updates, ready-to-use images, banner ads, press releases and other tools that make it easier for them to share and market your event.

To encourage speakers to appear at the event, you can offer them customized speaking opportunities that fit with your content and message yet highlight an area of their own expertise. Next, create customized promotional materials that spotlight their upcoming presentation. This makes it easier for them to promote and share your event with their own community of fans and followers.

You can also enlist your audience as promotional partners through "bring a friend" deals and affiliate programs. Here is one incredibly powerful, yet overlooked idea: Often, hosts do not look deep enough into the businesses of their audience. This is where many potential sponsorships or other opportunities may be hiding.

5. Establishes multiple income streams. At a live event, you can create multiple income streams including:

• Your own program offerings
• Back-of-room sales from guest speakers and strategic partners
• Sponsorships
• Repurposing products
• Other income generating opportunities

There are also hidden industry secrets to help offset event production costs. One of my favorites is using hotel points to purchase rooms for guest speakers and VIPs.

In addition to these five big benefits, you will also find that hosting your own live event grows your business by building your confidence, allowing you great opportunities to be featured in local media, giving you more ways to connect with your local community where your event happens and so much more.

Here are five steps to help you tie a live event to your marketing strategy—so you can grow your business with ease:

1. Create the theme and purpose of the event. The theme and purpose drives your event, your target audience, your partners. It also helps to determine the type of marketing channels to use.

Decide if you are holding a one-, two- or three-day event and what kind of content you will be delivering.

Give some thought to the overall experience you want your attendees to have. Be clear on why you are doing the event in the first place so that every decision you make is done "holding" the vision for your event. For example, are you doing the event for lead generation, to create awareness, to develop loyalty, to form partnerships, to fill coaching programs, to showcase a new product or to reach a larger audience?

Remember, if your event is not well thought-out, planned for and executed correctly—your expertise, passion and vision will not provide your attendees the transformation in their lives and business they have come to you to obtain—you may end up losing money.

The goal, of course, is to stay ahead of clients and competitors while providing the ultimate event experience within your budget. With careful planning and smart guidance, you can create that experience—and make a profit.

2. Select a date and location. The venue selection is probably the most important aspect of holding a live event. Careful thought needs to be given to whether the event is held in a hotel, conference center or community center. In general, holding an event at a hotel allows for maximum comfort and ease for attendees and can create a wonderful experience.

The location and quality of your venue is important to the attendee and to any VIPs, speakers and sponsors you align with to help you with marketing. A reputable location, with good pricing, great service and a wide range of facilities is most desirable.

It is wise to explore various possibilities and remember that you want to hold your event where it is most convenient to the largest part of your target market.

Some event locations you may want to consider:

• Atrium of a large commercial building
• Business center or conference room
• Church
• Community or convention center
• Cruise ship
• Golf or country club facility

- Historical site
- Hotel
- Library meeting room
- Museum
- Planetarium
- Poolside
- Resort
- Restaurant
- Sports complex
- Theatre
- University campus
- Winery
- Your place of business or home
- Zoo or other attraction

Get creative and look outside the box. Check with local chambers of commerce and visitor convention bureaus in your target city for additional resources and potential sites.

Be flexible when choosing your date. For example, peak seminar seasons are between March and May and again from September to November. Consider holding an event during the other months and look for locations that offer greater discounts to keep your budget in line with you goals. Give some thought to holding your event in the off seasons, when hotels offer better deals and packages.

3. Decide on your target audience. When planning a live event, many of us think we have to have a big audience. Not so. Whether you are planning for 10 or 1,000, taking the time to define your target audience helps you focus on meeting the group's needs. Rather than trying to make your content and vision fit everyone, focus on those you will best serve and who need what you have to offer. Form a clear picture of your audience. Consider age, gender, education, occupation, income, ethnicity, location, attitudes, values, habits and risks.

Build on the relationships you have first. It is okay to start with a smaller, intimate group, however if you are ready for a bigger crowd—go for it!

4. Decide on strategic alliances (speakers and sponsors). Be sure to invite speakers and sponsors who align with the vision and purpose of the event and who also bring a caliber and reputation to the event that provides the participants with relevant information to their work, industry or business.

5. Advertise and market the event using a variety of channels. With effective marketing, you can get numerous people to attend your event. You might include:

- Email campaigns (your own lists)
- The use of social media sites, such as Twitter®, LinkedIn® and Facebook®
- Strategic alliances
- Joint ventures
- Attending other live events yourself. Making those important contacts helps to spread the word about your event. Self-marketing is a great way to reach potential clients and fill your event.
- Webinars or teleseminars
- Blogging and guest blogging
- YouTube® videos
- Interviews on Internet radio stations
- Affiliate contests
- Give-aways
- Article marketing
- Donations to local charities in exchange for promotion

Now that you understand the importance of holding a live event, how it can benefit your bottom line, and have reviewed a few steps to get you started, remember that all events require a good team of people handling a variety of tasks to ensure you, the host, are able to be the star and focus on delivery and content.

Putting on your own live event is a very rewarding experience and does not need to be an expensive undertaking. Consider working with a professional event manager. Event organizing is a skilled profession and a great event manager will help free up your time so you can:
• Focus on attracting clients and participants
• Create your presentation and content
• Be more creative, productive and focused

In addition, a professional event planner will save you time, money and energy.

When you seek out and consult with a professional meeting manager, you are taking the first step to creating a purpose-driven presentation that will bring you personal rewards and profit.

Linda Cain
MCE OnSite
Turning ordinary events into
Extraordinary Experiences

626-974-5429
lindacainoffice@gmail.com
www.mceonsite.com

Linda Cain has been planning meetings, conferences and events for more than 25 years. Her passion to serve others, easy-going personality and a love for the meeting industry, have given her an edge in the field, resulting in her being a highly sought after independent meeting and event manager. To enhance her meeting business, Linda completed her Certificate in Event Management and also became a Certified International Etiquette Consultant with the renowned Protocol School of Washington®.

Working with individuals, speakers, coaches, entrepreneurs, corporate clients and non-profit associations has been a rewarding experience and has allowed Linda to build a terrific team. Linda is lively and energetic, and her "do whatever it takes" attitude is contagious. Based in Southern California, and willing to travel anywhere, anytime, Linda incorporates her meeting skills and etiquette training to provide her clients with the most in professionalism, style and attention to detail. She owns her own company, MCE International, as well as a live event support company, MCE OnSite.

When not managing meetings or providing live event coaching, Linda loves spending time with her family and friends, likes to read, water ski and raise Pomeranians.

Build Your Public Speaking Business with Ease

Generate influence, awareness and clients

By Anastasia Schuster

Public speaking is one of the most effective means to grow your business, period. Allow me to share with you why I strongly believe it belongs in every marketing tool kit, as well as my suggestions on how to get yourself booked and keep getting booked.

First, a success story: Tara is a sustainable farmer who came to me because she needed to grow her Community Sustained Agriculture (CSA) membership. Her members receive a weekly box of her meats and vegetables and are the primary source of revenue for her farm. Within a six-month period, I booked her 25 free speaking engagements, or gigs. As a result, 52 families came out to tour her farm. Of those families, 14 became CSA members, spending an average of $240/month. That does not include those who did not become members, yet purchased food at her farm store. Nor does it include those who continue to buy food from her store, farmers' markets and referrals who go on to become members.

Can you see the incredible benefit to Tara going out and educating people about sustainable agriculture? Her business has boomed as a direct result of her public speaking and she has educated more people about the need to eat "real" food than she ever could have done just by doing farm tours alone.

You might be thinking, *Well of course, she has a huge target audience because everyone eats, whereas my business is highly specialized.* True, however not everyone is willing to spend that much money to get her high-quality foods. This means her potential target market is not as large as you might think. Having said that, through her public speaking efforts, Tara has informed people as to why eating sustainably is so important. This has actually grown the size of her potential market. Do you see how much effect you can have in your own industry if you just get out there and educate others?

It does not matter what your business is. If you sell widgets, you can use public speaking to educate people as to why they need widgets in the first place. If you do it well, with integrity, and you do it to bless your audience with information—not "pitch" to them—your audience cannot help but want to buy from you. Public speaking establishes you as the expert, and people like to buy from those whom they like and trust.

The key is in the delivery. Though technique is important, it is the intent behind your message that will make or break the effectiveness public speaking has in growing your business. You have an expertise, a passion, a message to share. Though your ultimate goal is to get new clients, make the sharing of your story and making a difference in people's lives be the primary drive behind your presentations. Do that, and trust me—business growth will follow.

Think of public speaking as sample advertising, which is one of the most effective marketing tools out there. People will get a taste for who you are and what you do.

Another great benefit is that public speaking increases your "Google®
juice." In other words, you and your business will rank higher when
people search on your topic or industry. This is especially important if
you are an emerging speaker on the path to becoming professionally
paid. These days, nearly every group or organization will have an
online calendar, e-newsletter and other online resources that will
mention you. This is forever archived on the Internet.

*Okay Anastasia, you made your point, but I am not a great speaker and
I do not know where to begin to find speaking gigs.* I can understand
how it might be a daunting thought to add public speaking to your
marketing plan, therefore let me break it down for you. Trust me,
you can eat this elephant one bite at a time.

First let me explain that there are two primary types of speakers:
speakers doing marketing speeches—usually free—to grow their
business and professional speakers for whom public speaking is their
primary business.

This chapter is geared more toward the former, though the latter will
benefit if they are emerging speakers who understand the need to
pay their dues on the free circuit first. This helps them hone their
skills and increase their exposure, both of which can only be done
with a lot of experience.

I also want to clarify the difference between a program chair or
speaker coordinator and an event planner. The vast majority of your
free marketing speeches will be made to venues that already exist for
groups that meet on a regular basis. The people who book the speakers
are usually referred to as program chairs or speaker coordinators.
Event planners, on the other hand, are tasked with creating a specific
event, usually a larger meeting or conference. If they need speakers
they will do the booking themselves or task it to someone on their

team. Because I am focusing on marketing speeches in this chapter, and for the sake of simplicity, I will use the term program chair.

"You can speak well if your tongue can deliver
the message of your heart."
—John Ford, English 17th-Century dramatist
and playwright

You Want to Speak, Now What?

Here are some of my tried-and-true suggestions to get started.

- Brand yourself as a speaker. Be certain it is on your business cards, website, LinkedIn® profile, email signature and more. Think and act like a speaker in everything you do so it becomes a part of who you are.
- Create a speaker sheet. Keep in mind the purpose is to get you booked as a speaker, not to sell your products or services. If you are using an agent, be sure to have a second version, minus your contact information. This way leads go directly to your commissioned agent, not to you.
- Get the word out. Email everyone you know, share it via your social media channels, call friends and family and ask them for their support. Ask your connections for recommendations and introductions to potential program chairs.
- Start with the "low-hanging fruit" so you can have some immediate success. This will build up your confidence and experience. Local service clubs have a need for weekly or monthly speakers. Some of the best to reach out to are Rotary® International, Kiwanis® International and Soroptimist® International.
- Be clear on your target audience and think about where they gather. Do Internet searches for MeetUp groups, professional organizations and meetings where your potential clients gather. Find speakers you

admire who present similar topics. Go to their websites or get their speaker sheets to see the names of venues where they have spoken.

- Before approaching a potential group, do your homework. Learn all you can about who they are and what they do. Be familiar with where and when they meet. Reference this information when you communicate with them. This shows you have put some thought into this possible relationship. When emailing a potential program chair, introduce yourself and share what you do and why you feel your presentation will be beneficial to their group. Be sure to mention you have attached your speaker sheet.

- When the program chair expresses interest in your presentation, that is the time to ask important questions. Can you bring business cards, fliers and books to sell? Can you make an offer during your talk? Ask for the demographics of their group. This helps you customize your presentation to best meet the audience's needs.

- Be tenacious and creative. Often you will find a great organization where it is not clear who you should reach out to. In my experience, submitting generic requests through online contact forms are not effective. You need to email or call a person directly. The challenge is in finding the correct contact information, and it is not always clear who is responsible for booking speakers. Do not get discouraged, I encourage you to put on your Sherlock Holmes hat and think of ways to reach someone from that organization even if it is not the actual program chair.

- Most websites will list key names. If it is not clear who the program chair is, go for the president or head of the group. Look for them on LinkedIn, if they have a public profile, oftentimes they will have their email listed. If not, their website might have their email address or you might find it through a general Internet search. See if you have a common connection on LinkedIn who can introduce you. If you contact someone other than the program chair, be sure to acknowledge that you realize she is not the right person, but could she please facilitate a virtual introduction.

- Write a book. Authors and co-authors get more speaking gigs than other professionals. However, do not stop there, be certain your book has many great reviews on Amazon. With each book sale, ask the reader if she will take just a few minutes to give your book an online review. When I am vetting speakers who are authors, Amazon is one of the first places I look. You can bet program chairs do the same—that is why having a lot of positive reviews builds credibility.
- Be patient, often groups or associations are booking six months out—not to mention the fact that most program chairs have their own businesses to run. This means setting up speakers is something they do on the side. It might take a while to land the gig, and even longer before you can actually present. Do not lose faith—keep at it!

> *"It's much easier to be convincing if you care about your topic.*
> *Figure out what's important to you about your message*
> *and speak from the heart."*
> **—Nicholas Boothman, Canadian author**
> **and speaker**

Etiquette Goes a Long Way—Six Tips Your Mom Would Give You if She Were a Public Speaker

1. A few days before your presentation, send an email to reconfirm the date, time, place and your audiovisual requirements, if any. Also remind the program chair of the topic you will be covering.

2. At the same time, be sure to email the introduction you would like the program chair to use. This allows her time to practice reading it before the day of the event. Do not leave it to the program chair to prepare your introduction—after all, you know best how to sell yourself. Make your introduction brief; remember, it cuts into your

speaking time. Bring a copy with you in case the program chair forgets to bring her copy.

3. Once you have met the program chair and had a chance to test the audio/visual (A/V) equipment, get sociable. Meet people and memorize at least five names. Think of a way to address them during the presentation by name and mention something that shows you were listening to who they are and what they do. This not only allows for interaction, but whenever you remember the name of someone it shows them and everyone else in the room that you care about them.

4. Meet with people after your presentation. People are often intimidated to reach out to the speaker. Make yourself approachable—you never know where a new relationship might lead.

5. Even if you collect evaluation forms, email the program chair to ask if she would write a testimonial about your presentation. You can also ask if she would be willing to facilitate an introduction to another organization where she feels you might be able to speak.

6. Send a thank you note to the program chair. Though you may have spoken for free and might not have acquired much business from it, you still want to be gracious and acknowledge the opportunity. Good etiquette will go a long way, as the program chair may recommend you to another group for a future gig.

> *"It usually takes me more than three weeks*
> *to prepare a good impromptu speech."*
> **–Mark Twain, American author and humorist**

The Art of Speaking and General Presentation Tips

Here are eight important points to help you become a sought after speaker with ease.

1. Improve your technique. Knowing your subject matter is not enough to win over your audience. I would encourage you to hone your presentation skills so people will be clamoring to give you their business.

There are a plethora of resources. Toastmasters International® has a club in nearly every city. Seek professional training in workshops or one-on-one. Watch and listen to DVD's, books and online training. Consider YouTube® or Ted.com talks for training videos and examples of great presentations. Join the National Speakers Association.

2. Practice, practice, practice and then practice some more.

3. Remember Murphy's Law. By nature, I tend to be a Pollyanna, however when it comes to technology, I live by the rules of Murphy's Law. This means you can count on technology to let you down. Even if the program chair is providing a laptop, projector and screen, it is still best to bring your own equipment—including your presentation on a thumb drive—as a backup. Do not count on Wi-Fi working. Practice your presentation without A/V support so you can deliver it confidently should the equipment fail.

4. Imagine the mistakes. Run through all the scenarios that can disrupt your talk, such as a mobile phone ringing, someone choking on their food, loud noises, questions midstream, hecklers and people who highjack the conversation. Practice in your mind how you will handle these situations, so that if they happen, you will not lose your groove.

5. Study the audience. Do your research so you know what their interests are. This helps you tailor your talk to them. Also, learn their language. This helps you communicate effectively. Finally, dress appropriately, yet be yourself.

6. Pretend. I encourage you to resist the temptation to say you are nervous, are new to public speaking, are running on very little sleep, or—horror of horrors—did not have time to practice your presentation. Instead, exude extreme confidence in your ability as a speaker. Even if you do not feel that way, pretend. To be completely honest, I would rather chew on glass than do a public speech. No one would know that though, because I pretend. I pretend I am an amazing speaker because the growth of my business depends upon my presentation skills, and so does yours.

7. Be engaging, interactive and ask questions. Having high energy is pivotal to a successful presentation. I think we have all been through presentations where the speaker had less personality than a wet noodle. It is painful to sit through those! Here is how to avoid that problem: connect with your audience—do not just glance over their heads, meet their eyes and hold onto them one by one so everyone feels you are speaking to him or her. Be riveting!

8. End with a call to action. Be sure to end your talk with an opportunity to connect with you further. Do not make this a long sales pitch. Focus on delivering good content, and then spend just a few minutes on a low-cost offer. End by thanking the audience for their time.

> *"The eloquent man is he who is no beautiful speaker, but who is inwardly and desperately drunk with a certain belief."*
> **—Ralph Waldo Emerson, American essayist, lecturer and poet**

Make the Decision to Do it

Public speaking is fun, exciting and can be very profitable. There are so many experts who can support you in getting started, whether you need help updating your image and your website, or just need help creating great speaker and offer sheets. There are even experts who can help you develop your presentation and nail your delivery.

You can find a list of qualified resources on my website www.accessspeakers.biz.

If all this is rather daunting to you, just know that the time and effort you put into it is absolutely worth it. Remember how I told you that public speaking does not come easy for me? I feel the fear and I do it anyway. Why? Because I have a message, one that can make a difference in people's lives. If I do not get out there and speak, then how can I bless people with what I have to share? You too have a message, a passion and an expertise! Let that be the driving factor for you. Whatever may be holding you back—fear, lack of time, uncertainty—just get out there and speak. Think of all the people you will bless because of it and just do it.

Anastasia Schuster

Access Speakers

A high-touch speakers' agency...getting you
booked to grow your business

707-217-1252

anastasia@accessspeakers.biz

www.accessspeakers.biz

With more than thirty years of experience in the tourism industry, Anastasia Schuster has gained vast event management experience and been involved in more conferences than she can count. Her sales, marketing and PR know-how helped her build credibility with international suppliers whom she helped grow their businesses.

Through creating women's retreats and organizing social media conferences, Anastasia has first-hand knowledge of the other side of booking speakers. She speaks the language of program chairs and event planners who are tasked with finding great speakers for their venue. Anastasia's business model is unique compared to traditional speakers' agents who only represent paid speakers. She discovered there is a huge need from people speaking solely to grow their business, as well as emerging speakers who are not paid enough to garner representation from a traditional agent.

It pleases Anastasia to know that she is helping people grow their business, brand themselves as speakers and spread their message. Anastasia is a dynamic speaker herself. She speaks regularly on why everyone should use public speaking to grow their business as well as her time-proven strategies on getting booked.

Igniting a Fire for What You Do

The keys to going "viral" with ease

By Joe Hunnicutt, CTACC

Have you ever been around someone whose positive personality totally picked you up? Most of us can think of at least one particular person who is almost always enthusiastic every time you see them. It is interesting how just being around this kind of person can completely change your own disposition after being around them for even a short period of time.

It seems like certain people have a special spark of something that just makes them infectious. You could say that their enthusiasm really is contagious, right?

Now, think about what you could do if you were able to harness this sort of ability and deliberately focus it within your business. Can you imagine the power you would wield once you figured out the secret to "infecting" everyone around you to absolutely fall in love with your business, service or product?

It is worth pondering, *What is the secret to getting my goods to go "viral?"* Is it really just a random accident? This chapter aims to define how you can find a formula that allows your business to go viral with ease.

Where Do We Start?

Rather than spend time on the technical aspects of how to shoot a picture or video or write a blog post or anything like that, let us get to the essence of what makes some things catch on over all the rest. Really, what even makes us "contagious" in the first place?

We can get a hint if we go back to your enthusiastic friend. You see, if you simply take that word enthusiasm and break it down to its root meaning, you can get an idea of where this mysterious power comes from. In the original Greek word, where we find the root of the word enthusiasm, you will find the word *en-theos,* which literally translated can mean "inside god" or "having a god inside."

Rather than make this all about religion, let us look at the meanings behind the words and consider how they give us insight into this en-theos concept.

Think about it this way, when you are enthusiastic about something, you are usually pretty fired up about it. You feel good, energized and excited and it usually takes control of you to the point where you have got to share it with someone else, right? Therefore, the idea here is this: when you learn to tap into this power that is bigger than yourself and a source of unlimited energy and excitement, the natural by-product is that you become contagious with your overwhelming enthusiasm for what you are doing.

This is exciting, because once you figure out how to deliberately tap into your own en-theos, you have discovered a secret weapon for fueling a fire that can catch on with everyone around you and even take on a life of its own.

It all starts right here, right now, with you. However, it only works *if* you take the time to genuinely put these principles into practice. This is the starting point for every single coaching client we work with so that we can guarantee their results will happen fast and really last.

> *"When you discover your mission, you will feel its demand.*
> *It will fill you with enthusiasm and a burning desire*
> *to get to work on it."*
> **—W. Clement Stone, American businessman,**
> **philanthropist and author**

Clarity, the First Key Component

Learning how to intentionally focus your en-theos requires mastering three key components. First, it is very important to master your *clarity*.

The potency of this principle comes from understanding what it really means to have clarity in your business and especially when we learn how it relates to another word for clarity—*lucidity*.

You might recognize this word if you have ever heard of "lucid" dreaming. In case you are not familiar with the idea, this simply means you are fully aware while you are dreaming and in control of what happens. The science behind this says that lucid dreamers have a greater chance to exert some degree of control within their dreams and can manipulate the experience.

You can probably imagine the benefits of fully controlling your dreams. What fun! But do you realize this same principle can apply to your waking existence and your business?

Having absolute clarity is the first component that allows you to tap into your en-theos. Once you gain this clarity in two very important areas, you have the beginnings of what it takes to manipulate your experience in your business.

What exactly do you need to have clarity about? Well, for the purpose of fueling your fire, the first area has to do with your *why*. There are entire books written on this subject and the concept has been around for countless years. However, for whatever reason, it is also the one area people seem to lose sight of and not maintain, which ultimately leads to discontent and burnout within the ranks of most entrepreneurs.

Do you know *why* you are in business? Now, this is not about superficial surface elements we write down to make our business plans sound good. Why do you do what you do? Are you completely connected to that answer?

The people who do big things in the world around us, who have the tenacity that carries them through whatever this world throws at them, know this answer. They know their *why*. Do you? (See Mary Botham's chapter, *Cultivating the Mindset of An Entrepreneur with Ease* on page 23.)

If you are not completely clear on your *why,* then I have a gift for you. You can download a free series of exercises that will help you walk through this process right here: www.freestylestrategies.com/findingwhy.

Second, you need to be crystal clear about *what* you do. We are not talking about the perfectly polished elevator pitch you use with other professionals or the masterfully manicured marketing lingo you use with your prospects or clients. Rather, this is referring to the value you add to the world by *what* you do.

As you probably already know, you do not increase sales by simply spouting off features to people. You win their hearts by being the best one to explain the benefits, right?

First, however, you have to understand exactly what you do on the human level for another person by delivering those benefits. Do you know? Have you taken the time to find out? Once you have gained clarity and become fully lucid about *what* you do and *why* you do it, you will be amazed at the natural by-product that comes through in the sincerity of your tone and the lengths you will go to make things work.

The answers you find will fuel you and feed you and will infect everyone around you once you learn how to convey them just as clearly as you comprehend them in your mind. People love to support integrity. They love to be a part of something that is authentic because it feels good.

> *"Enthusiasm spells the difference between*
> *mediocrity and accomplishment."*
> **—Norman Vincent Peale, American minister and author**

Commitment, the Second Key Component

The second key component that is necessary to turn what you do into something contagious is your ability to master your *commitment*. You are probably already aware of the importance of this trait in business and how you need to be persistent and consistent with perseverance and determination. All these big words say the same thing. For our purposes, let us focus on what you are committed to so that you do not end up mistaking your activities for accomplishment.

Before we go any further, we should address a problem we are all dealing with nowadays that kills the productivity of even the most committed among us. You see, we are all overwhelmed by the tsunami of attention-getting media like no other time in history. It is really no wonder everyone around us is borderline ADD these days. We have been programmed to stay on the edge of our seats by all of this outside stimulus begging for our attention every second of our waking life. This is why the way you measure your commitment is by *your ability to minimize your distractions on a daily basis.*

The people who have figured out how to powerfully persuade those around them have dialed in their commitment and know exactly what activities to work at on a daily basis, as well as what activities to minimize so they maintain their momentum around what matters most.

They have figured out their "daily drivers" that feed them and fuel their fire just by doing these things every single day. Do you know yours? This is an important part of what magnetizes influence: everyone loves to be around people who not only love what they do but particularly the people they can count on.

If you are like most other entrepreneurs, you may have to struggle sometimes to stay committed. It is nothing to be ashamed of, as long as you have a system to get yourself back on track. This is where your clarity can support your commitment.

Consider this: How can you make your strategy—what you are trying to accomplish in your business—and your tactics—how you get things done—tie directly into your *why?* When you bring the power of your *why* into the function of how you get business done, you will find your commitment becomes second nature. The results that have possibly eluded you until now become a natural by-product of simply following through with all *your* "daily drivers."

By engineering your strategies and tactics to be in line with your *why,* you will not only have fun getting things done, you will make your mission irresistible to those around you who are craving some consistency of their own.

> *"Flaming enthusiasm, backed up by horse sense*
> *and persistence, is the quality that most*
> *frequently makes for success."*
> **—Dale Carnegie, American writer and lecturer**

Confidence, the Third Key Component

The last key to keeping your fire burning bright so you can light up the world around you comes down to mastering your *confidence.*

The importance of your confidence is certainly nothing new. All the great gurus have written volumes on how vital it is to every aspect of your business. Besides, you probably already know from personal experience how erosive a lack of confidence can be on your attitude and energy level.

This is actually one of the core reasons countless entrepreneurs throw millions of dollars every year into untold numbers of trainings and tools. It is to add something to their business that will give them just a little more confidence in doing what they do.

However, we are really missing the boat when we think that some "thing" outside of ourselves can create *lasting* confidence. That is what all those gurus are counting on though, that you will eventually come back, ready to throw more money at your problems. This is why it is so valuable to invest in your own confidence generating systems.

For right now, you will want to focus on just two areas that will secure your confidence and make it serve your purposes. There needs to be a constant stream of confidence in Number One, yourself, and Number Two, what you do—your business, product or service.

The secret is to make sure you are feeding your confidence in both areas on a *regular* basis. It seems like we fall into a trap of just building up our confidence completely in the beginning, thinking once is enough. The next thing you know, you are scrambling around trying out another one of the latest and greatest systems or doohickeys to compensate for the confidence you may have lost along the way.

There are actually several exercises for improving your confidence that I use with my coaching clients. However, right now our primary goal is to see how these three components fit together to ignite your en-theos and keep it raging for the purpose of influencing as many people as possible to "catch on" to your fire.

For this to work, you need to fully understand the power of your confidence. It can make you impervious to discouragement and setbacks, as well as empower you to get more done in less time with faster results. Your confidence can conquer hesitation and add a tone of sincerity that cannot be bought or learned.

When you take this knowledge and add to it the understanding that, deep inside, almost every one of us is secretly dying to be led, then you have found your formula for influencing your following.

It is easy to understand that those who master their confidence in self and in what they do will always have the attention and devotion of others because basically everyone loves to feel reassured.

"Enthusiasm is the mother of effort,
and without it nothing great was ever achieved."
—**Ralph Waldo Emerson, American essayist,**
lecturer and poet

Put it All Together

Now that you can see what these three key components are and how they support each other, things are going to get exciting. You now understand that you must have this fire for what you do, why you do it and how you do it before you can ever expect anyone else to have a fire for it, too.

By regularly investing your time and energy into the activities that reinforce your confidence, clarity and commitment, you will not only fuel your own fire, you will now have the formula in place to start igniting a fire in others for what you do.

This process has nothing to do with certain people being born with success in their DNA or only the "educated" having the upper hand. It also has nothing to do with some magical mysterious secret you have to spend good money to buy, or destiny or fate.

It simply has to do with the design of who we are and how we tick.

Once you put your understanding of your en-theos into play with your business model and all your interactions going forward, you will start to notice a profound change in the results you will be getting.

Because you exude **confidence** in your words and deeds, the natural result will be that people will believe in you and what you do and they will want to support your cause.

Because you are totally **committed** to every task you take action to complete, you will earn the loyalty of everyone you encounter because the world around you is hungering for reliability.

And finally, because you continually convey certainty by your crystal **clarity** in what you do and why you do it, you will be able to command a faithful following from those who are looking for this same elusive element in their own lives.

Tapping into your en-theos will give you access to an endless energy source. It will accelerate everything you attempt to accomplish in your business by providing you with a reliable resource for leveraging your efforts through others who catch on to what you are doing.

From lead generation to client retention, you can amplify the results of everything you do once you have harnessed your en-theos. From now on, you will not be constantly investing in tools and systems to compensate for any lack of clarity, commitment or confidence inside yourself or your business model. This is just another one of the immense returns on your investment in finding your fire.

Going "viral" is not a matter of making everyone love what you do. It is simply a system that compels people to share something with others and the truth is this, we share about the things we care about.

Since your business is merely an extension of you, the way you get your business to experience explosive growth is by first and foremost finding your fire. Next, follow the formula I have outlined in this chapter to fan those flames and give life to your en-theos. This is how you give meaning to what you do, and that is really what we are all looking for at the end of the day. It is certainly something worth caring about and even sharing about.

You now know what it takes to begin igniting a fire for what you do and ultimately make it go viral *with ease*. If you would like any help in this process, please drop me a note at joe@freestylestrategies.com. Helping others find their fire and monetize their passion is what I do.

Joe Hunnicutt, CTACC

Freestyle Strategies: The Blueprint to Live Your Life the Way You Want

530.913.9827
joe@freestylestrategies.com
www.freestylestrategies.com

The foothills of Northern California's gold country is where Joe and his wife call home. They live on a 500-acre ranch situated right next to the Yuba River.

Through the process of starting, building and even selling different service-based businesses over the years, Joe has learned what it really takes to launch a business that ensures your success in the shortest time possible.

As a Coach Training Alliance® Certified Coach, Joe specializes in showing solo-preneurs how to start, launch and grow a micro-business that will actually let them live their lives the way they want. Having years of "in-the-trenches" experience has earned Joe expertise in the variety of tactics it takes to make a business succeed with ease.

Whether he is working with you one-on-one or in his group coaching clinics, or even speaking to large audiences, Joe makes it his personal mission to help you find your fire. This is the foundation of what Joe calls "Freestyle Strategies." It is also the name of the coaching company he founded to help people like you become successful "lifestyle entrepreneurs."

How to Get Unstuck, Know Your Worth and Build Your Business with Ease

By Stacy Monroe

I t took an intervention from my three children for me to realize I had let things go for too long. They reminded me of who I was. How I built the business, what it used to be like. The last ten years had been rough. I went through a tough three-year divorce, an audit with the state of California and a two-year lawsuit that ended up in arbitration. The arbitration did go in my favor. Combined, these three incidences cost me more than $200,000 and left me feeling a bit deflated.

I had a hard time showing up for people at my business. I was more fear-based rather than trusting. I had stopped hiring staff, worried I would hire the wrong people. I had lost all my enthusiasm for my business, and it showed.

In life I could handle a failed business, however I could never handle letting my children down or quitting on them. I needed to find my way back—for them. I am smart and driven. I know what hard work is. I left home at the age of 16 with a one-month-old baby. She is now 32 and we work together. My youngest daughter works with me as well. My middle daughter lives in Los Angeles. During their intervention with me, I was so proud of them. I realized what a great job I had done raising them. They were so strong, compassionate and kind. It took me a few days to truly understand the impact that conversation had on me.

I had been stuck for too long. It was time to get un-stuck. I decided to jump back into my business, change it into the kind of place where I wanted to be. Not just for me, for my coworkers who depended on me. We were a team and they looked up to me. I had slowly stopped leading them.

Before that night, I had thought about selling the business, telling myself I was bored and frustrated. The income was down due to my lack of leadership, something I am really good at. Instead, I sat around comparing my business with others I looked up to. I gave myself every excuse in the book—why I could not be as good as the competition. I did some blaming—it was the economy, it was the younger generation's work ethic.

After the intervention, I thought long and hard about why I could not be like the salons I looked up to. At that point, what I needed to do was simple. I realized I was already halfway there. My staff was great. The bad apples where gone. The salon was beautiful. It was me who needed to show up. I had to learn to trust myself again.

This is what I did to become unstuck: I began to visualize the kind of salon for which I wanted to be known. I imagined myself working in it. I made a list of every detail—the sounds, the clientele, the products, the sales, the staff, the tone, the buzz. I described how we all felt working there, together as a team again.

I used to go to other salons to get my hair cut to see what other owners were doing. Some salon owners were nice enough to give me a tour and answer some questions. Other salons in my area opened and closed within a few years. Now that I am back on track, I am still standing after 19 years.

What makes me so different?

Sometimes we focus on what is wrong rather than all that is right. That can create problems. I recently asked a handful of good friends to write testimonials about me. These were for my eyes only. I asked for nothing negative—we already have enough of that in our heads. I was looking for some positive truths about who I was. Some of the words they used to describe me were passionate, trusting, encouraging, inspiring, generous and understanding. Their words validated me. I gained new strength from this exercise.

Before my salon and my successes of today, I was a young mother. No role models, I learned to take care of myself at an insanely young age. That being said, sometimes we do not acknowledge our accomplishments. If we are lucky enough, the people closest to us can help us find our way. Sometimes we have to find it on our own. I have always used public figures as mentors. I had many childhood issues that needed to be healed and spent years in therapy. Everything we do to succeed takes great effort. It is hard work.

I have done massive amounts of journaling over the past two decades. I recently read through some of my writing and noticed a pattern. I wrote the same things over and over again. It was all about this poor girl who was abandoned, neglected and abused. The truth is, I am not that child any longer and have not been for a long time. I no longer need to focus on the past. I had no control over it, so why let it affect me now? My childhood does not define my adulthood. Maybe subconsciously I was keeping myself down with all those excuses...

who knows. However, what I do know is this, I am done with all that. My story can be told by who I am today and my accomplishments.

Find Your Inspiration

I am a huge fan of Anthony Robbins. He is an entrepreneur, author and calls himself a "Peak Performance Strategist." I went to his *Unleash The Power Within* four-day workshop last year, and highly recommend this experience to everyone. It is life changing. He will help you shift your life. You will have huge breakthroughs regarding some of your negative beliefs. You will leave a different person than who you were when you walked in. In order to achieve that shift, you have to go all in. I went with a friend and we did not sit together on purpose. If you sit with someone who knows you, you may not open up as much. I shed a lot of tears and lost my voice. Without this workshop, I would not be this far in my personal growth, which is very important when you are a leader. Anthony Robbins inspired me. I encourage you to find the mentor, the workshop, the what and the why that inspire you.

Create Your Space

The first thing I do when I wake up in the morning is experience gratitude. I love my bed. My room surrounds me with things I love. I have framed pictures of my trip to Italy, my children and my granddaughter. There is a pastel painting of me meditating on a mountaintop, photographs and books. These are the things that remind me of who I am, why I am. Find ways to help yourself feel good the moment you open your eyes.

Hire the Experts

During my journey to jump-starting my business with ease, I hired a coach for the first time ever, Caterina Rando, MA, MCC. Working with her in a group setting has been one of my top five life-changing experiences. During the process, I realized I could not upgrade my life and business alone. I was ready to experience true success in my life. I was ready for 100 percent in all areas, my personal life and my business. My confidence was boosted back up to where it used to be. Caterina's expertise helped me become clear on what I needed to do to grow my business back to where it was and even better.

Make Lists

My vision was easy. I had years of secret crushes on other salons. I made a list of every area of my vision. I immediately had twenty things to do. I made another list, outlining what it would take to bring this vision to life. My third list was my goals. Next to each goal, I wrote ways to achieve them. My Number One goal was to double all the revenue generated in my business.

In order to know where you need to go, you must first know where you are. I like to start with easy, short-term goals. For example, if you average a sale of one bottle of product a day, your new goal is to sell two a day. This seems attainable. Another goal was to get more people to my social media pages, as well as into the salon.

If you are not using social media, then it is time to start using Facebook®, Twitter® and Instagram®. Add social media buttons to your website. You can also advertise creatively. I recently put a business card sized ad in my local paper, saying, *Be our new "like" on Facebook and automatically be entered into our monthly free giveaway.*

We keep track of each month's new "likes" and then hold a monthly drawing and post the winner on Facebook. If you have a retail store or referral partners, your sales rep can also sponsor you for some prizes. They will be happy to help.

Clean Up Your Space

I needed to clean up distractions around the salon. A few years ago, I started a traveling boutique. Eventually, I stopped doing the traveling boutique parties and incorporated the boutique into the salon. I thought it would be an easy way to make extra money. I did make a few bucks, however it was more of a dilution of the salon and spa experience. I am not letting this dream go, I am just shifting my goals. At some point I will do an eBay® store for my boutique.

Once I was clear with my "lists," it was time to make a list for my co-workers. I planned a meeting to get everyone to my house for a workshop. I put together a questionnaire so I could see where each person was. During the meeting, I added monthly incentive prizes on top of commission checks. Now we have first, second and third place winners each month. I also set a dress code for the salon.

Other improvements include blogging, videotaping before and after shots of our clients and sharing them on YouTube® and social media spots like Facebook.

We have two televisions in our salon. I have an in-salon commercial in production, showing all the services we offer at Stacy Monroe's, along with some "hair tip clips" from our stylists.

Focus on Details

Sometimes while implementing our systems, we find they are not as productive as we thought. When this happens, we may tweak the new system. When you are trying new things, it does not always work as planned and you can change it up.

For example, when I first implemented our dress code, it was an interesting experience. We call our dress code being "camera ready" and then I learned everyone has her own idea of what "camera ready" is.

Are you camera ready? If someone visits your place of business, even your website, are you showing your best self? I told my staff not to be surprised if one day a camera crew comes in to see what we are all about, because we have gone "viral."

One of my first steps during the "getting un-stuck" phase was staffing up. I was under-staffed because I was afraid of hiring the wrong person. I made a list of what I was looking for in a candidate. This way, during the interview process I could be clear on whether the person was a match or not. This strategy helped me hire who I was looking for.

All that hard work and careful interviewing paid off. Today I am super proud of my staff. I believe each and every one of them is a leader. I have accustomed them to having a leadership role by putting a different person in charge each week. This heightens awareness and gives each a different perspective when it comes time to being accountable.

Now that I have the right staff, I want them all to give the best impression. The stylists dress to impress. Our massage therapist and estheticians are in uniform. I made all my treatment rooms consistent with each other. I created first-time client "Welcome" incentive packets, which include an invitation—and a discount—to entice individuals to come back and try a different service. I also redesigned my brochures, cards and gift cards.

One thing I am most excited about is launching my own skin care line. My struggles with skin care lines in the past have been flaky sales reps and the fact that every other esthetician has her own favorite products. As in most businesses, you cannot afford to change your skin care lines or core products often. It is very expensive. I think I have done it about ten times over the years. I have done my research and know what my customers need and want. It is time to have my own line. Where in your own business can you create a highly customized product or specialty?

In this fast-paced world we live in, I find people want instant gratification. I have to admit, I have fallen into this category at times. I have to remind myself to breathe and slow down. This is why yoga has been a good match for me. What can you do to ease your mind when you are feeling stressed?

I have a calendar with a list of what I need to do that day. I have added in yoga four days a week, along with grocery shopping. If you are going to eat healthy, you have to be prepared. Am I perfect? No. Do things come up? Absolutely! If I need help, I delegate or add it to my list for the next day.

Final Suggestions

These are some of my successful business changes that might also work for you:

- I made our referral program quick and easy. For each new client you send us, you receive a free service.
- I suggested all co-workers have a kick-butt business card. I tell them, everywhere you go, hand some out.
- Start up conversations about what you do.
- Make a first time offer potential clients cannot refuse.

My staff and I agreed to meet every month for six months to work on our short-term and long-term goals. It is something we had never done, yet felt it necessary to make real changes. This extra investment in the business, in my team, has really paid off. Our revenue goals are on track.

Get Un-Stuck with Ease

Find your experts! Set your goals. It is how you will get unstuck in your business and proceed with ease. Get clear on your vision. Make your lists. Prioritize your lists. Fill out your calendar. Having your calendar will help you stay on task. Write down what you will be doing each day. This way when you wake up you will know exactly what your daily plan is.

Staff up or "re-staff" with people who are committed to your vision. If you do not have a business coach, get one! For those big changes you will need help. If you do not get it, you may fall off track and do what you always do, and keep getting those disappointing results.

Get on a healthy diet. You will need to feel good everyday. If you have a poor diet, you will not have the energy for yourself, your plan and the people involved.

Have a staff meeting, except call it a "Staff Workshop" and make it exciting. Open some champagne and put on some music. Get excited about where you are going. This is infectious.

Do not have any doubts about what you are trying to achieve. Even if you have a virtual team, find a way to have fun and keep them strong in your vision. It is how you build your business, discover your value and re-engage your sense of play, all with ease.

Stacy Monroe
Stacy Monroe's Salon & Spa

510-537-8084
stacymonroesalon@yahoo.com
www.stacymonroes.com

Nineteen years as a business owner has taught Stacy Monroe many lessons. Stacy first started doing hair at the age of 17 as an assistant. Today she has worked her way up to the owner of a twenty-chair, six-treatment room, three-manicure station, full-service salon and spa. Another division of her business is a traveling boutique, as well as a mobile airbrush tanning service. Where Stacy sees an opportunity, she takes it.

Through Stacy's knowledge, she inspires others to live their lives to their highest potential. Stacy teaches women to go out and get it by asking them, "What are you waiting for?" She excels at helping them solve what keeps them from achieving their ultimate goals.

Stacy's own personal life story is inspiring. She knows first-hand how difficult it is to stay on top. She helps clients create the systems that need to be in place in order to succeed. Stacy also believes that getting to know people's stories is how you build strong relationships. Stacy is looking forward to being a stronger voice and is excited about moving into a stronger position as a "go-to girl" for many more entrepreneurs.

How to Develop Group Programs that Catapult Your Revenue

By Caterina Rando, MA, MCC

I imagine that because you are reading this book you love your work and I also assume that you would like to share your value and serve more people. Perhaps you would even like to serve a lot more people. When you have a business that provides one-on-one service, you cannot grow your revenue beyond a certain point without adding new products and services.

If you are leading a workshop, webinar or are delivering a speech, you want to always provide massive value to the participants and then invite them to do more with you. This next invitation is called an upsell. One of the best revenue streams to add is a group program because it provides great value and is more affordable to the client. Plus there is a huge bonus to the people in a group program—they get to connect with other like-minded people who are working on building similar skills. The community you create for them allows them to gain additional support, advice, opportunities, trusted alliance partners and even clients.

You do not have to get tons of training or a certification to start providing group programs. For example, if you are an image consultant you can lead a group for women and teach them how to create their own personal sense of style. If you are a productivity coach, you can educate your group about best practices, then guide them into implementing the strategies that will work best for them.

Starting a Group Program with Ease

I started my group programs in a very unexpected way. I did not have a master plan; I came up with an idea and tried it out. Fortunately it worked. I have since learned a lot about running group programs that I want to share with you here.

Some years ago, I was preparing to lead a teleclass on the topic of growing your business with ease for women business owners from all over the country. I was only being paid $100 for the call and I was thinking about what I could do to further monetize—make money from—the opportunity. I decided I would offer a 12-week group program called Business Breakthrough. I did not have an outline or an offer sheet, a webpage or even a place online to take payments. I simply made the offer at the end of the call and asked people to email me if they were interested. I told them I would call them in the next few hours to answer their questions and get them registered. For the next four hours, I talked to women business owners and signed them up for the class. I had thirteen ladies in my first Business Breakthrough program—I felt like I discovered the secret to massive monetization!

I love leading group tele-programs and if you are not doing it already, the time to start is now. Not only is it wonderful to have clients all over the world and to serve them without leaving your house, it also leverages your time and allows you to catapult your revenue. I tripled my revenue when I started offering group tele-programs. Today I also offer live and in-person programs and elite mastermind groups. The possibilities of what group programs can do for your business are endless. If you wait to get started, you put off earning the revenue these programs will generate. I always tell my clients, *do not wait until you are ready, take action when you are willing.* If you are willing—and I am hoping you are—what follows is how to get started with a group tele-program. Then we will talk about live and in-person programs, too. I have so much for you. It is time for us get started!

How to Run a Tele-Group

One big challenge about a tele-group is that people cannot see you and you have to work harder to keep them engaged on the call. At the start of every call, have members announce themselves. This way you can acknowledge them for being there and it also lets you know which clients have joined the call. I also make a list of names of listeners so I can call on someone if no one speaks up when I ask for shares. It is worth noting that people will be more engaged if they have heard their own voice on the call. This is why you want to always have an interactive call.

Group size determines the format for the call. If you are doing more coaching and consulting, you will want to keep the size small, say a maximum of twelve people. If you are holding more of a training session, with questions at the end of every call, you can go bigger, up to thirty people.

Get Started with Group Tele-Programs

Tele-programs are the easiest way to begin because they cost you almost nothing to hold and you can go forward even if you have a very small group.

Super Tip: The best way to fill your paid group call is to hold a free telecall. This is a short call, designed to get people interested in signing up for the paid program. The focus of this free call is not sales—save your "ask" for the end of the call. Be sure to provide excellent content and value to your listeners. This sets the stage for what they will receive on the paid call. A great free call proves your expertise and shows that you will deliver what you promise on the paid call.

How to Create and Run a Group Program

Decide on the format and schedule of your group
Two things you need to decide on is the format and scheduling frequency. Is this a smaller group with lots of interaction or a larger group where you are sharing more information and there is less time for discussion? You need to clearly communicate the objectives to the group so participants know what to expect. As far as scheduling goes, whether you meet weekly, bi-weekly or monthly is determined by the content you deliver. You need more time between calls if you coach on business development strategies and less time if you teach a skill like how to use social media.

Here are a few other questions to consider:
What is the focus or purpose of the group?
Is it a support group, a mastermind group, a group of people coming together to learn a new skill from you? Do your clients want to focus on a particular objective like growing their business, improving their health or using social media to build their list?

Is it going to be a group that meets weekly, monthly, bi-monthly, quarterly or longer?
Once you know your purpose, you can determine how often you want the group to meet and for how long. Here is another super tip:

start with a shorter period of time. This means do not launch a year-long program when you have not yet had a six-month program. Do not create a twelve- or sixteen-week program when you have not even done a four-week program.

How many people do you want to have in the group?
This will largely be determined by the format of the group and the information you plan to share. For example, a mastermind group has a lower number of people because you need plenty of time to shine the spotlight on each person. If your group is mostly you teaching and there is time for questions, then you can have a much larger group.

What kind of group is it going to be?
A support group is a gathering of people who want to benefit from connecting with others having similar experiences. Topics covered could be professional or personal. It could include anything from a grief support group to a single mom's support group to a group for couples who want to adopt a child to a group for people trying to lose weight. You could be the facilitator of a support group. You do not have to provide content nor solutions.

A mastermind group is a small group, no more than 12 participants. These people come together to focus on improving a particular area of their business. During the meeting, you speak with each participant and offer solutions to keep them moving forward. At the end of the meeting, group members say what actions they will take before the next meeting. This promise adds an accountability element to the group. As the leader, you facilitate the group and its discussions. You can also provide content although that is not mandatory.

A training program is another kind of group that can be large or small. This is a group for learning new concepts and skills and you share a lot of content. It is key to providing several different ways of learning: discussions, partner and small group exercises for example. Keeping the learning interactive makes for a more successful training.

A train-the-trainer program is a group set up by you to teach others to do what you do. Like a training program, these groups can either be large or small. These sessions are also content-rich and focused on particular learning outcomes that you outline in advance. In this case, people are being trained by you to go and train others on what you have taught them.

What is going to happen in your group?
Before you begin marketing your group, decide what content you will to cover. Even if the group is a support or mastermind group and you are not planning on delivering content, you still have to decide what will happen at each meeting. Will you have everyone introduce themselves? Will the group have exercises to complete in class, group discussions, sharing from each participant? To enhance what you come up with, survey your clients and ask what they want to gain from a group. Pay attention to the questions your clients ask and the challenges they have. These are all possible areas for you to explore in your group.

Where and when will your group meet?
Once you know your strategy, you can decide when to hold your first session. Then you can take the necessary steps to fill the program. I encourage you—once you have these questions answered—to start marketing. Do not wait until your content is developed or all the other details are in place. When clients tell me they want to start a group, I tell them to *pick a date and pick a place and get going*. This is a very important idea and I want to explain why.

Too often, I see entrepreneurs waiting to be ready before they begin. Please note that "being ready" is a myth and a lie we tell ourselves.

It is only in the deciding and then the doing that we become ready. Also, your first group is rarely your best one or your most profitable. When you hold your first group session, pay attention to what you want to do differently the next time. Keep upgrading your program until you feel it is outstanding.

How to Add Value to Your Group

Treat your group members like VIPs and they will tell their friends about you and your programs. Here are some ideas that make people feel special—and add value to your group programs.

Support your group with a private Facebook® group. This is an easy way to build your online community. The bonus for members is they get access to exclusive content and ongoing support.

- Whether you are socializing online or on the group calls, support members by encouraging them to share their successes and then give them an opportunity to promote what they are doing to build their business.
- Facilitate them getting to know each other, encourage them to support each other and spend time connecting outside of normal meeting times.
- Add a bonus monthly call. You can interview experts, answer specific questions or provide additional coaching for those who need it.

How to Price Your Program

Pricing your program is different for everyone. I cannot give you a blanket statement that says *this kind of program should cost x and that kind of program should cost y*. Instead, let me give you some guidelines to consider. First you have to look at your costs related to both marketing and delivering your program. If your program is virtual—delivered online—your costs will be lower. Therefore, your price can be lower, too. If you host an in-person program, it will have higher costs. You can charge more for an in-person program than a virtual program.

I always recommend that my clients start with an introductory price, one they believe will fill their first group. Then the price goes up as they become more confident and have a successful track record.

How to Market and Fill Your Live and In-person Group with Ease

Tele-groups and webinars or other virtual groups are great places to start and I want to take a moment to tell you how holding a live and in-person event will catapult your business even faster and with ease. Here are a few super tips to make your live event successful. (Also see Linda Cain's chapter, *Using Events as a Marketing Strategy to Grow Your Business with Ease,* on page 177)

- **Hold a free teleclass or webinar.** This is a great way to fill every program—new or ongoing—with ease. People are curious about what you have to offer, therefore show them how much value you have to bring.
- **Create a special landing page** on your website that includes information about the program and links to register. Use this as a way to capture names and build your mailing list for future events.
- **Plan a special live event**—for your live event. It is harder to fill the room for a one- or two-day event. You can do so with ease by holding a workshop or other introductory event. This gives people

a chance to meet you personally—always a good thing—and learn more about what you offer and what they will gain by joining you. Then at your live one- or two-day event, offer your group program.

- **Make a list of all past clients** you think would be great for the group. Reach out to them—your personal invitation can generate more sales than a series of free telecalls or email blasts.
- **Use email blasts** to get the word out. Use your newsletter to invite people to your free telecall or webinar. Once they register, use email blasts to remind them of when the call takes place. After the free event, email them to encourage registration. Once they have signed up for your paid program, use email blasts—also called auto-responders—to remind participants when the group program begins. This last step also generates excitement and gets them ready to consider future programs.

Catapult Your Revenue with Group Programs

You have so much value to bring, so much information and knowledge to share. Holding telecalls, webinars or live events are amazing ways you can watch yourself amaze yourself. Group programs are just one way you can build community and reach your audience with ease. Here is another: I invite you to join me at my Business Breakthrough Summit. This two-day, live event is where I share more ideas that will catapult your business. You will discover how to build your client base and come home with what I like to call *now money now* and *more money later.* Join me at my next summit: visit www.bizbreakthrough. com. Use coupon code BSWE97 to attend the event for $97.00.

Caterina Rando, MA, MCC
Watch Yourself Amaze Yourself

415-668-4535
cat@caterinarando.com
www.caterinarando.com

Caterina Rando shows women entrepreneurs how to be loud and proud about who they are and the value they bring. For twenty years, she has shared her message of how women can succeed in business.

She is a master certified coach, business strategist and author of the national best-seller *Learn to Power Think* from Chronicle Books 2002, now published abroad in 11 languages, including Estonian.

Caterina is also the creator of two live events, *The Sought After Speaker Summit* and the *Business Breakthrough Summit*. Both two-day events are designed to catapult your business. To find out about these events visit www.soughtafterspeaker.com and www.bizbreakthrough.com. Use coupon code BSWE97 to attend either event for $97.00.

Caterina is also the founder of THRIVE Publishing®, a firm that publishes business books for entrepreneurs so they can grow their business. THRIVE Publishing is proud to have published this book.

In her spare time, Caterina focuses on the organization she founded called, A Good Deed Tea, whose mission is to raise money for education and entrepreneurship training for women and girls around the world.

More Business Success with Ease

Now that you have learned about many ways to build business success with ease, the next step is to take action. Get started applying what you have learned in the pages of this book.

We want you to know that we are here to help and inspire you to meet your personal objectives. The following pages list our geographical locations. Regardless of where we are located, many of us provide a variety of services over the phone or through webinars and we welcome the opportunity to travel to your location or invite you to ours.

You can find out more about each of us by reading our bios at the end of our chapters, or by visiting our websites listed there and on the following pages.

When you are ready for one-on-one consulting or group training from any of the co-authors in this book, we are available! When you call us, let us know you have read our book, and we will provide you with a free phone consultation to determine your needs and how to best serve you.

Geographical Listings for *Business Success with Ease*

Switzerland
Carmen Okabe   www.carmenokabe.ch

United States

California
Mary Botham	www.marybotham.com
Gloria L. Brown, CPPC	www.glospeaks2u.com
Linda Cain	www.mceonsite.com
Bibi Goldstein	www.buyingtimellc.com
Heidi Hoch, Commercial Broker	www.heidihoch.com
Joe Hunnicutt, CTACC	www.freestylestrategies.com
Candy Messer	www.abandp.com
Stacy Monroe	www.stacymonroes.com
Diana Concoff Morgan, MA, HHE	www.wholeheartmarketing.com
Caterina Rando, MA, MCC	www.caterinarando.com
Anastasia Schuster	www.accessspeakers.biz
Linda Sturdivant	www.nophonefear.com

Texas
Debbie Saviano	www.debbiesaviano.com
Kasey Roberts Smith	www.artistryofimage.com
Pam S. Russell	www.pamrussell.com

Nevada

Danni Ackerman   www.thedanniapp.com

Lynda Jean, MSW, AICI   www.lyndajean.com

Virginia

Patrick H. Ennis   www.incmarketingservices.com

Terry Monaghan   www.timetriage.com

About
THRIVE Publishing™

THRIVE Publishing develops books for experts who want to share their knowledge with more and more people. We provide our co-authors with a proven system, professional guidance and support, producing quality, multi-author, how-to books that uplift and enhance the personal and professional lives of the people they serve.

We know that getting a book written and published is a huge undertaking. To make that process as easy as possible, we have an experienced team with the resources and know-how to put a quality, informative book in the hands of our co-authors quickly and affordably. Our co-authors are proud to be included in THRIVE Publishing™ books because these publications enhance their business missions, give them a professional outreach tool and enable them to communicate essential information to a wider audience.

You can find out more about our upcoming book projects at
www.thrivebooks.com

You're Invited...

...to join us for any of our **Sought After Speaker Summits!** In one weekend you will discover how speaking builds credibility, generates influence and attracts more clients, quickly and easily. Join us for our next live event at: www.soughtafterspeaker.com. Use coupon code BSWE97 to attend either event for $97.00. We look forward to seeing you there!

...to join us for the **Business Breakthrough Summit**, where you will learn how to create new streams of income and establish yourself as an expert in your field.

Discover how to add clients with ease and how to be loud and proud about the value you bring to the marketplace. Find out more about our next live event at: www.bizbreakthrough.com. Use coupon code BSWE97 to attend either event for $97.00. Attend this event and watch your business thrive!

Get Published with
THRIVE Publishing

Become a Published Author with THRIVE Publishing…and start sharing your knowledge. We can help you become a published author to showcase your expertise, build your list and advance your business and career. Our experienced team makes the process fast, easy and affordable. You will have your book in hand sooner than you ever expected. We also partner with organizations or institutions to publish books that can be used to advance fundraising efforts or create additional revenue streams. Contact us to discuss how we can work together on *your* book project.

Phone: 415-668-4535 or email: info@thrivebooks.com

Other Books from
THRIVE Publishing

For more information on
Socially Smart & Savvy, visit:
www.thrivebooks.com/store

For more information on
Woman Entrepreneur Extraordinaire, visit:
www.thrivebooks.com/store

Other Books from
THRIVE Publishing

For more information on
Catch Your Star, visit:
www.thrivebooks.com/store

For more information on
Make Your Connections Count, visit:
www.thrivebooks.com/store

Other Books from
THRIVE Publishing

For more information on
Entrepreneur Extraordinaire, visit:
www.thrivebooks.com/store

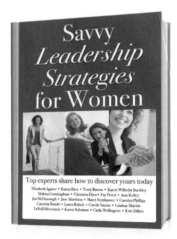

For more information on
Savvy Leadership Strategies for Women, visit:
www.thrivebooks.com/store

Other Books from
THRIVE Publishing

For more information on
Power to Change, visit:
www.thrivebooks.com/store

For more information on
Mom Entrepreneur Extraordinaire, visit:
www.thrivebooks.com/store

For more copies of this book, *Business Success with Ease:*
Top experts share strategies for accelerated growth
contact any of the co-authors or visit
www.thrivebooks.com/store